KNITTING FOR TOMMY

Keeping the Great War Soldier Warm

Lucinda Gosling
in association with
Mary Evans Picture Library

The History Press

First published 2014

The History Press
The Mill, Brimscombe Port
Stroud, Gloucestershire, GL5 2QG
www.thehistorypress.co.uk

British Library Cataloguing in Publication Data.
A catalogue record for this book is available from the British Library.

ISBN 978 0 7509 5596 6

Typesetting and origination by The History Press

CONTENTS

ACKNOWLEDGEMENTS

In the process of compiling this book, a number of people have generously shared their knowledge and deserve recognition. I'd like to thank vintage knitting expert Joyce Meader for her help and hospitality. The items she has collected over the years have contributed greatly to the interesting variety of images I'm able to share here, and I cannot recommend her enough if you yearn for your own First World War balaclava but cannot produce one yourself. I also would like to express my appreciation to Barbara Smith of the Guild of Knitting & Crochet, who read through the text and offered her comments. Barbara also contributed items from the Guild's archive towards the book. Other people who have shown interest and support are Peter Donnelly of the King's Own Regiment Museum, Linda Newington at the University of Southampton Library, Dawn Cole, Jenny Duff, Pauline Loven, Melanie Gall, June Holman, Neil Bloomfield, Alison Otterbeck and Kevin Ramsdale.

Will you join the Army of Women Workers who use

ARDERN'S CROCHET COTTONS?

The most noteworthy change that has arisen through the war is the adaptability of women to many kinds of work hitherto done by men.

A New Army — The Army of Women Workers —

has arisen, who find that the weariness of manual and clerical work is appreciably relieved by a change to the restful pastime of "doing a bit of crochet."

You do not have to tire yourself by walking from shop to shop to buy Ardern's Crochet Cotton, as every up-to-date Draper or Art-Needlework Dealer stocks it.

White, in all numbers, 00 to 60.
Colours, in number 8.

INTRODUCTION

KNITTING FOR TOMMY

In August 1914, the War Office was faced with the task of kitting out a volunteer army of an unprecedented size. In Great Britain, from July to September 1914, 253,195 men voluntarily enlisted and, by 1918, over five million British men had worn uniform.

In comparison to German soldiers, the average Tommy was well equipped. Throughout the war, British soldiers wore the khaki field service uniforms, based on the Pattern Service Dress of tunic and trousers introduced in 1902. Issue drawers, vests and flannel shirts, along with tunics, trousers and greatcoats (of which there was a shortage in the autumn of 1914) made from thick, unyielding rough woollen serge, provided limited protection but little comfort against the bitter cold and damp of a French winter. Military

Women adapting to 'all kinds of work hitherto done by men' in this advertisement for Ardern's Crochet Cottons.

overcoats and tunics could become depressingly waterlogged and hands needed warmth and protection while on front-line duty. Socks were allocated at a rate of three pairs every six months, amounting to 137,224,141 pairs issued to men over four years; an astonishing number, but still inadequate. Making do with just three pairs of socks in normal conditions might be manageable, but the misery induced by making do in flooded trenches and on endless marches can only be imagined. More seriously, spare, dry socks were imperative if the painful and debilitating condition trench foot was to be avoided. What British soldiers needed was comfort. And comforts they got.

On 29 August 1914, three weeks after the outbreak of war, Lady French, wife of General Sir John French, placed an appeal in *The Times*:

There is a great need for knitted socks, &c., for our troops. It is, indeed a crying need as the War Office allowance is only three pairs for each man, and a long day's march will wear socks into holes. I would ask those who have leisure to knit, or are willing to employ others to do so, to send parcels as soon as possible, not direct to me but to Miss Douglas and Miss N. Selby Lowndes at the Ceylon Tea Depot.

Lady French kept up her requests, and by January 1915 she was asking the nation's knitters to provide her with 300,000 mufflers, at the request of the War Office. *The Queen* magazine reported that:

As they are needed as soon as possible, no time should be lost in setting to work. Fortunately these mufflers are the easiest things in the world to knit, making the minimum of demand alike upon the skill, time, eyesight, or energy of the worker. Children can manage them quite well, and a fairly expert knitter finds no difficulty in completing one or even more in a day ... and of course, khaki is THE colour; so great is the demand for it, however, that some difficulty may arise in obtaining it or even the various brownish shades which are almost as effective; so it may be well to mention that different tones of darkish greys do quite well.

An army of women in silhouette sharing one huge ball of wool used as an incidental illustration for the women's column of *The Graphic* newspaper in 1915.

Dorothy Constance Peel, who, under the name of Mrs C.S. Peel, wrote the weekly cookery column in *The Queen* magazine, recalled the epidemic of knitting during the first two years of the war in her memoirs *How We Lived Then*:

We knitted socks (some of them of unusual shape), waistcoats, helmets, comforters, mitts, body belts. We knitted in theatres, in trains and trams, in parks and parlours, in the intervals of eating in restaurants, of serving in canteens. Men knitted, children knitted, a little girl promoted to four needles asked anxiously of her mother, 'Mummie, do you think I shall live to finish this

sock?' It was soothing to our nerves to knit, and comforting to think that the results of our labours might save some man something of hardship and misery, for always the knowledge of what our men suffered haunted us. It was said that such a stock of knitted goods flooded into the trenches that men cleaned their rifles and wiped their cups and plates with their surplus socks and comforters.

In its 'Court and Social' column, *The Observer* described the changes wrought on society by war:

> Dinner parties are extinct as the Dodo in this new London; people dine together in twos and threes, and bring their knitting ... It has been said of the Queen in old days that Her Majesty knitted at every spare moment: at meals, and in the evening when talking to anyone. This may now be said of the major portion of the social world of London; every woman knits and most of the men. Those who did not know before how to manipulate knitting needles have speedily learnt, and thousands of useful woollen garments – socks, comforters, belts and mittens – have been made in the West End and sent out to our troops in Northern France.

The Lady's World Fancy Work Book from January 1915 reminded readers not to forget about sailors in the Royal Navy, who were braving icy blasts out on the North Sea:

> With this need in view we are publishing a few articles which will give real warmth and comfort to the man at the

helm or the nimble sailor at the mast-head. At the present moment, we are working a scarf with the very nicest and softest wool which can be obtained, as we do not consider that comforts for either soldiers or sailors should be knitted with anything but the best wool.

It went on to recommend Faudel's A.A. Peacock Quality Fleecy Navy Blue Wool, knitted with a pair of No. 2 wooden knitting pins.

Knitting 'comforts' for troops was a tradition that harked back to the Crimean War in the mid-nineteenth century, and had continued half a century later during the Boer War, though the climate of South Africa did not necessitate woollen garments as much as the bitter cold of Sevastopol. But just as neither conflict was on the scale of the First World War, neither was the corresponding volume of knitting. Knitting for soldiers and sailors in 1914 became a national pastime – perhaps even a national mania. The outbreak of war, on an August Bank Holiday, had taken the country by surprise and, in the melee of mobilisation, the question of what Britain's civilians could do to help their fighting men found a quick and simple answer in a pair of knitting needles and a ball of wool. Appeals were published in the press, working parties were formed and women's magazines published patterns, often known as 'recipes', for a whole range of knitted garments to provide succour and comfort to men at the front. Knitted comforts soon began to be collected officially by various charities and organisations. Queen Mary's Needlework Guild, which produced an estimated 15.5 million separate items during the war, many of them knitted, requested that all donations be sent to the collection centre at Friary Court, St James's Palace. At Burlington House, home of the Royal Academy, the Red Cross occupied several galleries for their Central Workrooms, producing and packing a constant stream of surgical requisites and hospital garments. Locally, village groups and communities galvanised their efforts to knit

more fruitfully, while garments were collected at regimental level too. In early September 1914, Major General Babington of the 16th Lancers was writing to the press to request comforts for his men, as was Mrs Jasper Farmar, wife of Major Farmar, who was collecting for the Worcestershire Regiment. Lady Henderson requested caps, gloves, knitted jackets, wristlets and socks for men of the Royal Flying Corps out in the field.

Children learnt to knit too, as did wounded men in hospital, refugees, prisoners of war and theatrical celebrities. Imprisoned rebel women in Ireland were even set to knitting socks, and *The Times* commented how nannies and children's nurses were 'absorbed in knitting projects of a complicated kind'. One ingenious lady had begun knitting a scarf and left it, partially complete, in a railway waiting room, with a note for the next stranded lady to add an inch or two to the muffler; a system of combined endeavour that produced a respectable number of completed mufflers.

Soon, as Mrs Peel observed, it became *de rigueur* to take one's knitting around to dinner parties or the theatre, or even to the law courts. Among the various Christmas gifts suggested by *The Tatler* magazine in December 1914 was 'a useful knitting case' from J.C. Vickery's of Regent Street. 'As everyone is knitting just now,' it wrote, 'no apology is necessary for drawing attention to the knitting case fitted with excellent bone and steel needles, crochet and wool hooks.' Those who could not knit were urged, if they could afford to, to send wool to those who could. Lady Evelyn Templetown, wife of the 4th Viscount, organised a small company of

Advertisement for H.K. Wilkinson, Yarn Merchant of Accrington Road, Burnley, 1915.

A British soldier proudly displaying a knitted vest under his jacket, which, as well as keeping him warm, doubled as a portable chess and draughts board, according to *The Sketch* magazine in which this photograph was featured in 1915.

excellent knitters to knit socks for soldiers – one of whom, a blind lady, had knitted over 150 pairs in eighteen months.

Certain prominent figures also made the provision of comforts their wartime project. Mr John Penoyre, of 8 King's Bench Walk, Inner Temple, London, devised a scheme to provide sweaters for soldiers, publicising his appeal in a series of lively letters to *The Times* where he updated readers on the climate in France, the corresponding need for warm jumpers and the planning needed to provide such clothing before the advent of colder days. For those who questioned why the War Office could not provide for its own army, Penoyre provided the answer:

> Our men form the best equipped armies ever put into the field in the course of history, but that is not to say that it is for the Government to dress them up like White Knights to meet every possible emergency. The extras (the comforts, that is) are to be supplied as wanted by you, and it is to be your pride to do this ungrudgingly ... When you come to think of it, the technical use of the word 'comfort' is an addition to the vocabulary of the war, and it is instinctively a good one ... The fact is the human mind is so constituted that in times of very special stress and trouble the little extra personal comforts to which one is attached bulk very large indeed.

Penoyre also pointed out the gratitude of the recipients, emphasising that as well as the improved physical well-being brought about by comforts, it was the psychological boost of knowing that the thoughts and warm wishes of those at home were bound up in each row of stitches. It meant they were not forgotten. By September 1917, at the time of this letter, Penoyre's appeal had received 83,337 individual items, of which just about half were sweaters.

Sir Edward Ward (1853–1928), as Lord Kitchener's deputy in superintending the personal welfare of all overseas troops and also Director General of Voluntary Organisations, was responsible for encouraging the nation's knitters to keep up the momentum. In September 1917, after three years of war, he was writing to the papers again to stress that the urgency for comforts was as great as ever:

> May I, through the medium of your columns, urge all who can knit to make as many knitted comforts as possible (especially mufflers, mittens, helmets, and socks) for general distribution to the troops, in order that an ample supply may be available for dispatch overseas during the autumn and winter months?
>
> With our increased Armies the demand is almost overwhelming, and I appeal to all workers to make a supreme effort to enable me to meet it by knitting steadily for the next three months at least.

The need for men did not wane and, consequently, nor did the need for warm clothing and hospital garments. But many women, who had initially taken up needles at the outbreak of war, had moved on to find other ways to contribute to the war effort. In her famous memoir, *Testament of Youth*, Vera Brittain admitted she was 'utterly incompetent at all forms

The khaki puttee – one of the most ubiquitous items of clothing worn by the First World War soldier – was usually shop-bought, but knitters could always produce a homemade alternative.

of needlework, I found the simplest bed-socks and sleeping helmets altogether beyond me'. Instead, she trained as a Voluntary Aid Detachment nurse, working in hospitals in London and France.

Women's magazines also encouraged the nation to keep knitting, with a constant stream of advice and encouragement. *Woman's Own* ran a competition asking readers to knit socks and mufflers according to the magazine's published instructions. The knitter of the most perfect pair of socks received a not insignificant 20s first prize, while the best muffler was awarded 10s. Six runner-up prizes of 'lovely silver-plated hand-mirrors' were offered for the senders of the next best knitted mufflers and pairs of socks. The magazine assured readers that 'the Editress guarantees to distribute the knitted articles amongst soldiers and sailors really in need', adding that if any competitor knew of a man to whom she would like the knitting sent, she could attach their name, number and regiment to the item and the competition entry would be forwarded on, providing stamps were supplied.

The results of the nation's knitting endeavours were not always of such a high standard and the comic potential of the frustrated and inexperienced knitter grappling with purl and plain, and the bemused recipients of unrecognisable garments in the trenches, provided fertile subject matter for comic artists in magazines like *Punch* and *The Tatler*.

The Queen magazine published a letter from one reader in their 'Social Problems' column

MEN'S WEAR.

August.   February.

"*Dress does make a difference.*"

(an apparently genuine enquiry – *The Queen* did not joke about such things), who asked how she might delicately tackle one acquaintance's enthusiastic but sub-standard production of knitted socks:

A cartoon drawn by Captain J.H. Thorpe of the Artists Rifles for a YMCA fundraising gift book *Made in the Trenches*, reflects the contrast in clothing worn by British soldiers in the trenches in August and February. The soldier on the left wears the familiar khaki tunic, breeches and puttees. On the right, the man is swaddled in a goatskin coat with balaclava and scarf, very possibly hand-knitted 'comforts'.

> Mrs A, who is collecting comforts for soldiers, calls one afternoon on a friend Mrs B, who gives her a parcel, saying, 'I know you want more socks, so I have knitted these for you.' Mrs A thanks Mrs B and asks her to luncheon the following day, when they will look over the things and pack them, as they must be sent at once. Mrs A then opens the parcels and finds six pairs of socks all so badly knitted and so small as to be practically useless. What should Mrs A say or do?

Perhaps Mrs B's socks were some of those destined to clean rifles and boots in the trenches. At least then, her efforts were not entirely in vain.

However, though some socks might have one or two dropped stitches and some mufflers might unravel, the image of the British Tommy in the trenches, wrapped up against the cold in an array of helmets, balaclavas, scarves and sweaters, has become a familiar one. Around the globe, millions of comforts were knitted to warm both the body and soul of the fighting man, while thousands more volunteers collected, packed, raised funds and ensured a distribution network that delivered these homespun tokens of love and patriotism to those who, regardless of their sartorial merit, wore them and appreciated them.

The writer Jessie Pope is best known for her poetry during the First World War. Published in national papers such as the *Daily Mail*, her poems have been increasingly decried over the past century as propagandist doggerel, but alongside the blind patriotism Pope's prolific output touched on almost every aspect and experience of the war and her populist rhymes chimed with the preoccupations of a nation. Her poems 'Socks' and 'The Knitting Song', published in 1915, are, above all, an expression of how knitting connected the Home Front with the fighting fronts, both actually and metaphorically. When she wrote of Britain's women 'knitting love and luck in every row', she echoed the sentiments of many who poured their efforts into each and every sweater, hat or pair of khaki socks:

The Knitting Song by Jessie Pope, 1915

SOLDIER lad, on the sodden ground,
Sailor lad on the seas,
Can't you hear a little clicketty sound
Stealing across on the breeze?
It's the knitting-needles singing their song
As they twine the khaki or blue,
Thousands and thousands and thousands strong,
Tommy and Jack, for you.

Click – click – click,
How they dart and flick,
Flashing in the firelight to and fro!
Now for purl and plain,
Round and round again,
Knitting love and luck in every row.
The busy hands may be rough or white,
The fingers gouty or slim,
The careful eyes may be youthfully bright,
Or they may be weary and dim,
Lady and workgirl, young and old,
They've all got one end in view,
Knitting warm comforts against the cold,
Tommy and Jack, for you.
Knitting away by the midnight oil,
Knitting when day begins,
Lads, in the stress of your splendid toil,
Can't you hear the song of the pins?
Clicketty, click – through the wind and the foam
It's telling the boys over there
That every 'woolly' that comes from home
Brings a smile and a hope and a prayer.
Click – click – click,
How they dart and flick,
Flashing in the firelight to and fro!
Now for purl and plain,
Round and round again,
Knitting love and luck in every row.

1

KNITTING MATTERS

A ready-made cardigan, showed off proudly in this advertisement for London store Frederick Gorringe, published in *The Tatler* in November 1915.

For those who have tried and failed to master knitting, it is an acquired skill and one which, even in 1914, not everyone possessed. Those who were less than proficient at knitting could of course apply their energies elsewhere (in fundraising or in packing comforts for instance), but for those determined to complete a pair of socks, there was help available. Knitting lessons were arranged at schools (as evidenced in school log books from the period) and through the numerous charitable organisations set up to ensure the steady production of comforts. Yarn manufacturers and women's magazines printed articles and leaflets with helpful advice, including items that the less accomplished of knitters could perhaps achieve. Today, experienced knitters can spot a First World War knitting pattern due to the direction of the stitches – older patterns from the Crimean and Boer War eras work the garment from top to bottom, while First World War items were knitted upwards.

Advertisements for wool brands such as Cock O' th' North, Ladyship or Cockatoo took on a predominantly military character, urging magazine readers to select the very best quality for their comforts and listing a selection of uninspiring colours: grey, navy, 'drab' and, of course, khaki.

In February 1915, J. & J. Baldwin of Halifax, one of the country's biggest wool manufacturers, best known for their

Beehive brand, arranged for a qualified teacher of hand-knitting and crochet to be in attendance at the Art and Needlework department of Harrods so that 'ladies anxious to knit comforts for troops could receive instruction free of charge', together with a free leaflet. Publishers Dean's produced a special kit – the Man in Khaki kit – complete with tape measure and instructions for methodically knitting the perfect soldier's sock.

Other yarn companies produced pamphlets filled with patterns for comforts, and magazines dedicated to knitting and crochet, such as the snappily named *The Lady's World Fancy Work Book*, turned their attention to ever more inventive ways to clothe fighting men. *Leach's* magazine, published by George Newnes, produced one booklet offering two styles of knitted slippers for convalescent soldiers 'to help them keep their feet warm', including a checked beribboned pair specifically designed for Highlanders. Presumably, members of the flamboyant kilted Highland regiments would not be content with the plainer alternative! Comforts did not always end with the final casting off. In the case of trench hose – woolly leggings designed to be worn over socks and under boots as an additional layer – these were often soaked in linseed and then ironed with brown paper to give waterproof qualities; the resulting smell was probably insignificant compared to other smells suffered in the trenches.

Although many of the authors of these patterns remain anonymous, two particular experts in their field emerge during this period. Marjory Tillotson (1886–1965) was the chief designer for J. & J. Baldwin (the company would merge

Baldwin's advertising its 5-ply white heather Scotch fingering wool to make the anachronistic-sounding cholera belt, 'a great safeguard against chill from exposure and damp and also against intestinal orders'.

with Scottish firm Paton's in 1920) and produced most of their knitting publications from 1908 onwards, including the *Woolcraft* booklet, familiar in most British homes. In a career that spanned fifty years, Tillotson was the most influential designer of knitwear in England and could claim to have devised patterns through both world wars, often gleaned by researching patterns passed down through the generations by families or within towns and villages. The second designer of note was Henrietta Warleigh, the daughter of a clergyman, who had written several knitting books for the Society for the Promotion of Christian Knowledge in the latter half of the nineteenth century. *The Queen* magazine published a number of her recipes for comforts, several of which she gave her name to, including the Warleigh helmet – a kind of super-balaclava covering the chest, shoulders and head – and Warleigh leggings.

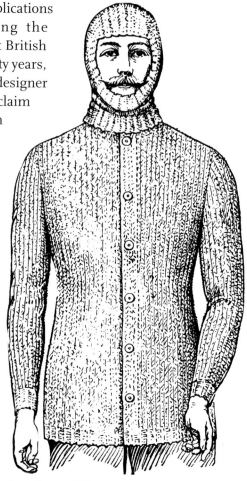

A SHETLAND WOOL CARD GAN
At Scott Ad e s

Knitters were asked to expand their repertoire beyond the usual comforts. Though not strictly a knitted item, after the use of gas at Ypres in April 1915, Harrods was soon advertising a list of available items with which to make respirators, including scoured wool.

Within weeks of the outbreak of war, the need for hospital requisites such as swabs, dressings and slings also became starkly apparent. The Kensington War Hospitals Supply Depot co-ordinated the vast number of contributions made from bed jackets to surgical stockings, as did various branches of the Red Cross. By January 1916, *The Queen* magazine was printing a pattern in response to an urgent appeal for operation stockings, to be knitted in white wool such as Paton's 4-ply fingering:

> Again and again our thoughts must turn to the wounded, and those of us who cannot give active service on their behalf welcome a way in which we can help at home, even by a very few hours' work. Such a way is provided in the demand for operation stockings, which is almost paralysing to those already engaged in the production of hospital necessities, so tremendous and apparently unceasing is the call.

As with food and many other commodities, Britain relied on foreign imports for much of her wool from New Zealand, Australia and South America, and even before the outbreak of war there were concerns about the country's wool supply. As early as January 1913, wool merchants at the Bradford Chamber

As the nation knitted socks and mufflers, shops continued to offer a wide range of woollen and fur-lined garments, suggesting them as ideal festive gifts to be sent to the front. This Shetland wool cardigan, with balaclava, was available from Scott Adie's of Regent Street during Christmas 1915.

SUGGESTED CHRISTMAS GIFTS FOR BRITAIN'S "BLUE" AND "KHAKI" BOYS.

CHAMOIS LEATHER WAISTCOAT.

Send for Christmas List. Price 6d. redeemable.

With long sleeves and back of same leather. Very warm and comfortable. Does not take up much room under jacket.

Natural Colour	... ...	**21/-**
In Brown Chamois	...	**25/-**
Extra long, in Dark Brown		**35/-**
Superior Quality, extra long, in Brown or Grey ...		**45/-**

SLEEPING CAPS.

The favourite Cap with men of both forces. Can be worn as ordinary cap or turned down over face and neck, as illustrated. In khaki or navy. Each **2/6** and **3/6**

CARDIGAN JACKETS.

Khaki Wool Cardigans. Medium and heavy weight, fine protection from cold. Price each **7/11**

Special Quality Cardigans for sailors. In Navy Wool. Scotch Make.

Each **7/11**

Grand Christmas Bazaar Now Open.

The FLANDERS WAISTCOAT.

A most comfortable garment for wear on active service. Can be worn open or buttoned up when required. Made in Fawn Fleece, light in weight, but snug and warm. **18/6 & 21/-**

Also made in Blue Fleece for Naval Officers. **21/-**

This waistcoat is also made in soft tan Leather, lined all wool. **50/-**

A. W. GAMAGE, L^D.. HOLBORN, LONDON, E.C.

of Commerce had been expressing concerns about wool supplies, due to increased consumption globally. In November 1914, the *Manchester Guardian*, which took a particular interest in the wool industry of the North, reported: 'The demand for an immense amount of khaki cloth has come at a very bad time for the trade, the supply of wool being very inadequate now.' The anxiety stemmed from the fact that the July clip from New Zealand had been used up and another clip was not due until January, after which there would be several weeks before the wool arrived in Britain. The paper reported that one solution was to buy the Argentine clip for £5,000,000, which would expect to land in Britain in the first week of January. By December 1914, with these unforeseen pressures on home-produced supplies, there was a serious wool shortage. Continuing problems of importing wool from Australia and New Zealand due to a shortage of dock labour, lack of berth space and difficulties of transport, meant that the supply of wool would be a constant source of concern throughout the war. The Government bought up large consignments from abroad for war purposes, and those who knitted through an officially recognised body such as the Red Cross could often be supplied with wool, provided it was returned in the form of complete knitted garments. Mr John Penoyre informed readers of *The Times* that 'recognized associations obtain wool at the Government price from any of the D.G.V.O.'s* depots through the country on the understanding that it is returned in the form of knitted comforts for the central pool'.

*Sir Edward Ward, Director General of Voluntary Organisations

'Suggested gifts for Britain's "Blue" and "Khaki" boys' from Gamage's, the famous department store in London's Holborn, with examples of the various shop-bought garments available for soldiers spending winter in the trenches.

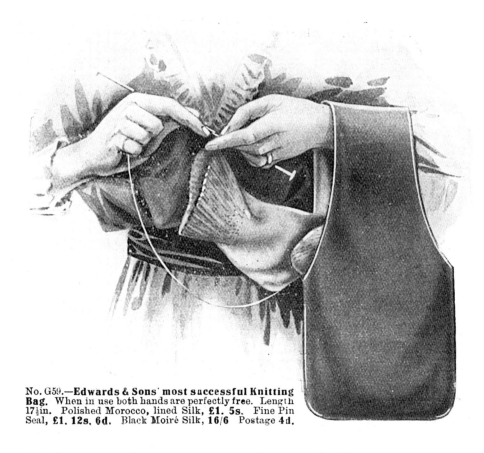

No. G59.—**Edwards & Sons' most successful Knitting Bag.** When in use both hands are perfectly free. Length 17½in. Polished Morocco, lined Silk, **£1. 5s.** Fine Pin Seal, **£1. 12s. 6d.** Black Moiré Silk, **16/6** Postage 4d.

This illustration in *The Queen*, on 20 November 1915, advertises Edwards & Sons' 'most successful' knitting bag, which, when in use, left both hands perfectly free to get on with producing comforts.

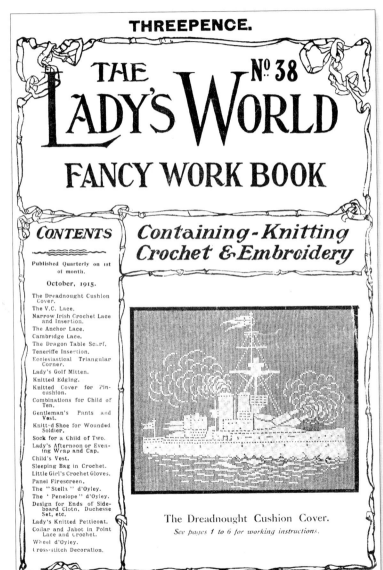

THREEPENCE.

THE LADY'S WORLD

Nº 38

FANCY WORK BOOK

Containing - Knitting Crochet & Embroidery

CONTENTS

Published Quarterly on 1st of month.

October, 1915.

The Dreadnought Cushion Cover.

See pages 1 to 6 for working instructions.

Front cover of *The Lady's World Fancy Work Book,* a good source for knitting patterns during the war. This particular issue features on its cover a design for a dreadnought cushion!

Perhaps the most curious response to wool shortages took place at Burlington House, home of the Royal Academy, where a new industry was started: spinning dogs' hair into yarn. There, under the auspices of none other than the British Dog Wool Association, ladies at spinning wheels worked with hair from Pekingese, chow, collie, Pomeranian and any other breeds prized for soft, silky hair. How the recipients felt about receiving a scarf of pure Pomeranian, or socks made from Samoyed wool, we can only guess at – and hope they were not allergic to dog hair.

Wool shortages required some enterprising ideas including this one – spinning dog hair into wool at the Red Cross Central Workrooms, Burlington House (home of the Royal Academy).

Advertisement for Cock o' th' North knitting wools made by Carter and Parker of Baildon Mills, near Shipley in Yorkshire, specifically promoting its wools for soldiers' comforts.

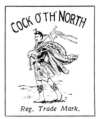

KNITTING WOOLS
For Soldiers and Sailors Wear

If you are making comforts (Helmets, Body Belts, Socks, etc.) for our soldiers and sailors, bear in mind that each article will have to stand hard wear, and that warmth is the great consideration. Only the best makes of wool will stand the strain or provide the warmth.

COCK O' TH' NORTH
BRAND.

The following makes are specially adapted for this purpose :

4-ply Super Scotch Fingering and Double Knitting

To be obtained from Dealers in Knitting Wools, Fancy Drapers, Art Needlework Depots, etc. :: :: :: Do not be put off with other kinds, but send us a postcard for the name of local dealer.

Made by
CARTER & PARKER,
Baildon Mills, near Shipley, YORKS.

Reg. Trade Mark.

One of the bibles of knitting during the First World War: the *Woolcraft Practical Guide to Knitting and Crochet* published by Baldwin's of Halifax.

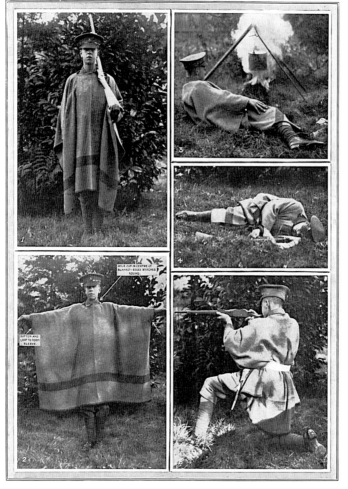

1. A BLANKET WORN AS AN EMERGENCY OVERCOAT BY A SENTRY.

2. HOW THE BLANKET IS USED AS AN OVERCOAT: A HOLE CUT IN ITS CENTRE FOR THE HEAD TO PASS THROUGH, AND THE SIDES HELD TOGETHER BY BUTTONS AND LOOPS TO MAKE SLEEVES.

3 and 4. THE BLANKET-OVERCOAT IN USE.

5. THE BLANKET-OVERCOAT LOOKING ITS MOST PICTURESQUE.

With "chill October" here, and a rumour that the demand for military overcoats may possibly, for the moment, rather exceed the supply, a timely and practical suggestion is made for the benefit of our soldiers at the front, and on duty in this country. It is pointed out that, with practically no damage done to it, a blanket can be turned into a serviceable and warm overcoat, which will not impede the movements. The instructions are very simple : Cut a slit in the centre of the blanket and stitch a herring-bone round. A button and a loop must be placed at each centre extremity to form the cuff. The weight of the blanket prevents it from blowing open, and the wearer, by placing his belt outside, can close the blanket up entirely, as shown in one of our pictures.—[Photographs by Clarke and Hyde.]

In the early weeks of the war, there was a shortage of military overcoats, calling for some imaginative makeshift garments such as this example, published in *The Sketch* magazine in its 30 September 1914 issue. The photographs demonstrate how to convert a blanket into a cape-like coat, secured with a belt when necessary.

Accessories to facilitate the knitting process became popular, such as this bracelet, which was able to suspend wool from the wearer's wrist allowing knitters to carry on, even on the move.

Frederick Gorringe's advertisement for knitting wools for the troops.

The Pool of Comforts

BEGIN your contribution to-day to the Soldiers' Pool of Comforts. Remember the men in the trenches still need socks, gloves, mittens, helmets, mufflers, and jerseys. Nothing is too good for them—and nothing is better than

PATON'S *Alloa* *Knitting Wools.*

Luxuriously soft and warm, they stand the hardest wear. Remember that supplies of wool are growing scarce—order, therefore, what you require at once.

In Khaki, Navy Blue, Drab, Natural, Grey, and in all colours. Patterns of wool free on request. "How to Knit Soldiers' & Sailors' Comforts" sent for 1½d. in stamps.

PATON'S, ALLOA, SCOTLAND; also at 192, ALDERSGATE, LONDON, E.C. 1.

Knitting comforts was only one aspect of the process. This Paton's advertisement shows a group of women cheerily packing up items for distribution overseas.

Paton's advertisement with a young girl showing a patriotic interest in her mother's knitting. The text underlines the importance of buying British: 'because their manufacture keeps thousands of Britons in employment; because buying Paton's Wools you support a thoroughly old-established British industry.'

It's really a double delight to use Paton's Wools for 'Comforts'

It's a delight because Paton's Wools are such a treat to knit with, so soft and warm in wear, so splendid for standing rough washings & hard usage.

It's a delight again because Paton's Wools are British through and through; because their manufacture keeps thousands of Britons in employment; because buying PATON'S WOOLS you support a thoroughly old-established British Industry.

PATON'S
KHAKI KNITTING WOOLS

Select Paton's Super and Rose Wheelings, Paton's Rose Petticoat, Paton's Super and Rose Fingerings or Paton's Double Knitting —all will make 'Comforts' for which our Soldiers and Sailors will be grateful. Paton's Wools are obtainable everywhere.

NEW BOOK "*How to knit Soldiers and Sailors' Comforts.*" *Fully Illustrated. Sent free for 1½d. in stamps. Write to-day.*

PATON'S, ALLOA, SCOTLAND, ALSO 192, ALDERSGATE ST., LONDON, E.C.

Printed for the Proprietors by OD. A CHAS. STRAKER, Ltd., 12-15 St. John's Square, London, E.C. Sole Agents for the Colonies— GORDON & GOTCH, Ltd., London, Australia, Canada, etc. Sole Agents for South Africa—THE CENTRAL NEWS AGENCY, Ltd.

Wholesale Trade Agent—B. HARDBOROUGH & Co., 51 Old Bailey, London, E.C. Rates and Terms for Advertisements upon application.

'The Knitting Needle has again come into its own.' Front cover of a small booklet published by the Higbee Company (USA).

Right: Pictured outside an army tent, the comforts worn by these two soldiers on the front cover of a Baldwin's leaflet look somewhat bizarre, but were no doubt effective for guarding against the cold.

Knitted COMFORTS FOR MEN on LAND and SEA

Made from

J. & J. BALDWIN'S

TRADE — MARK

"WHITE HEATHER" SPECIALITIES

J. & J. BALDWIN & PARTNERS LTD. HALIFAX ENGLAND.
ESTABLISHED 1785

:: OUR KNITTING COMPETITION ::

First Prize, £1 for Socks ; 10s. for Muffler

SIX BEAUTIFUL SILVER-PLATED HAND-MIRRORS

If you can knit, you can do your country a service at the present time, for there is constant appeal for warm comforts from the men in the trenches and the sailors on board our ships.

What are needed most are good mufflers and warm socks for the Army and Navy, and in order to encourage our generous-hearted readers to supply the needs of our brave men in the fighting lines, we are offering most handsome prizes for making mufflers and socks to our patterns.

For the best pair of Knitted Socks (made to our instructions) we offer the sum of

TWENTY SHILLINGS

and for the best Knitted Muffler (made to our instructions)

TEN SHILLINGS

Should the Editress decide to divide the prizes between two or more competitors sending in pairs of socks or mufflers equally as well made, she reserves the right to do so. The knitting will be examined by experts, and the prizes awarded to those competitors entitled to them. The Editress's decision must be accepted as final. In addition there will be

· LOVELY SILVER - PLATED HAND - MIRRORS

given as Second Prizes to the senders of the next best knitted mufflers and pairs of socks.

A form bearing the competitor's name and full address must be attached to each pair of socks or muffler sent in. The Editress guarantees to distribute the knitted articles amongst soldiers and sailors really in need, but should the competitor know of any man to whom she would like the knitting given, she may attach his full name, number, and name of regiment to the article, and it will be forwarded direct, if stamps are enclosed to cover the postage abroad.

"Woman's Own" Patriotic Knitting Competition

NAME..

ADDRESS..

....

Jan. 8th, 1916

The knitting must not be sent in until February 2nd or later than February 8th, the closing date of the Competition. Further particulars will appear next week.

❄-❄

INSTRUCTIONS FOR KNITTING THE SOCK

Materials required : 5 ozs. of grey or khaki 4-ply fingering, and 1 set of No. 13 needles.

Cast 28 sts. on 3 needles, making 84 in all. Work 45 rounds of 1 pl., 1 p., which makes grip for leg. Now change to 3 pl., 1 p., and work until 10½ inches in length from beginning.

Commence heel by placing on one needle 22 s. each side of a p.s. Keep this p.s as seam st. (s.s.) for heel. 39 s. are now left on the other two needles. Slip the 1st s. on needle set for heel, p. back, knitting s.s. plain. Work 36 rows of pl. and p. alternately, always reversing the s.s. and slipping the 1st. To turn heel :

1st row : K. 22 s., k. s.s., k. 1, sl. 1, k. 1, bring sl.-s. over, k. 1. T.

2nd row : Slip 1st s., p. 4, p. 2 tog., p. 1. T.

3rd row : Slip 1st s., k. 5, k. 1, bring sl.-s. over, k. 1. T.

4th row : Slip 1st. s., p. 6, p. 2 tog., p. 1. T.

Repeat these rows, knitting an extra s. each time before narrowing, until you reach either end of needle, when 25 s. should be left. K. back, then place 12 of these stitches on one needle, leaving 13, and pick up 19 loops from side of heel. Place all the stitches for front of foot on one needle, and work along, always keeping pattern for front, as before. Now pick up 19 loops from side of heel and place on the other heel needle. Work round to end of front needle, then commence gusset.

K. 1st s. on next needle, sl. 1, k. 1, bring sl.-s. over, and k. round until within 3 s. at end of next needle, (Continued opposite.)

2

KNITTING ROUND THE WORLD

The *Woman's Own* patriotic knitting competition, offering a whole 20s as first prize for the best-knitted socks.

Great War knitting was not exclusively the preserve of the British. The front cover of *L'Illustration* magazine, France's leading illustrated weekly, for 24 October 1914, carried a drawing of a tranquil scene in a French cottage, with three generations of women – grandmother, mother and daughter – engaged together in knitting by firelight in a scene of determined, familial industry. Another picture, a photograph published several times in the British press, depicted a group of women busily knitting in a dimly lit wine cellar in the bombarded city of Rheims. Nothing, not even German guns, could stop the click of French knitting needles.

Around the British Empire, people were taking up their needles with equal gusto. *The Times* reported in November 1914 that the 'women of Canada of all sections and classes are knitting, knitting, knitting and joining with eager enthusiasm in every project to supply comforts to the Royal Navy and British Armies in the field'. The Associated Field Comforts society, part of the Canadian War Contingent, was formed specifically to distribute comforts to Canadian soldiers in France and began to supply knitting machines at a local level in order to increase production. In one month alone, the city of Hamilton in Ontario sent 27,892 pairs of socks to the front. Each parcel was received, together with a cheery letter from active volunteer Marion Simpson, notifying soldiers that the garments were produced via the association and not as official rations. The addition of some friendly tidings alongside these hand-knitted gifts helped to boost morale among the homesick and lonely, and numerous soldiers began to correspond with Ms Simpson, expressing their thanks for the kind words and encouragement she had sent with the socks. Also in Canada, the Duchess of Connaught, aunt by marriage to King George V, had taken possession of a knitting machine at Government House in Ottawa, with which she had, according to the report, made over 1,000 pairs of socks for Canadian soldiers. She was pictured in *The Bystander* magazine working away at it in early 1917, just a few months before her death in July. In India, too, people set to work, where branches of the Imperial Indian Relief Fund formed working parties to sew and knit for troops.

The output of Australia and New Zealand, unhampered by the wool shortages affecting Europe, was particularly impressive. The Australian Comforts Fund, whose motto was

Illustration by C.E. Peto in *The Sketch*, 4 August 1915.

Love's Labour

The Vision Feminine

'Keep the Fit Man Fit', produced an incredible 1,354,328 pairs of socks during the war. The wife of the Governor of New Zealand, the Countess of Liverpool, compiled *Her Excellency's Knitting Book*, containing directions for a variety of comforts, with all profits from the publication going to the St John Ambulance base hospital. In its preface, the book promised: 'it will prove a useful friend to the knitters and workers in New Zealand who are working on behalf of our soldiers.'

In the United States, even before their entry into the war, there were efforts to do something to help the Allies in France. Female American passengers on board HMS *Celtic* in October 1914 spent their passage to England knitting socks, jackets and mufflers for British soldiers, a large stock of which was handed over to the purser on arrival for transfer to the proper authorities, and it was reported that several church ministers in New England had invited women of their congregation to carry on with their knitting during the sermon. By the middle of 1917, the United States was 'knitting for Sammie': children in elementary schools were taught to knit via Red Cross programmes, university

British soldiers assembled in a room at Soltau
prisoner of war camp, Germany, 1918; note the
soldier in the foreground who is knitting.

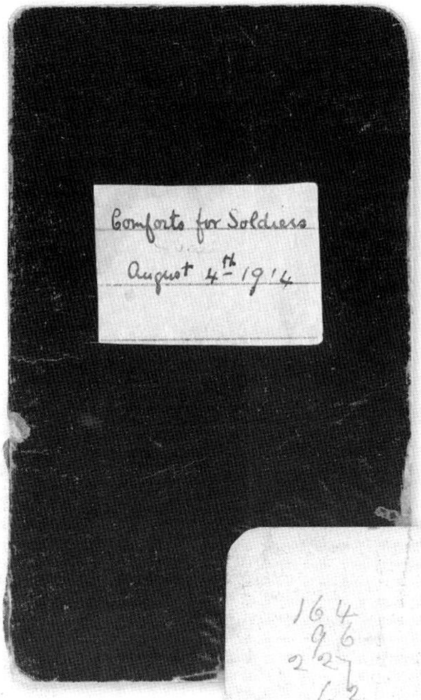

A small notebook in the collection of the National Army Museum records comforts collected by an unidentified community together with the items' destination units.

Astonishingly, the first consignment is noted down on 4 August 1914.

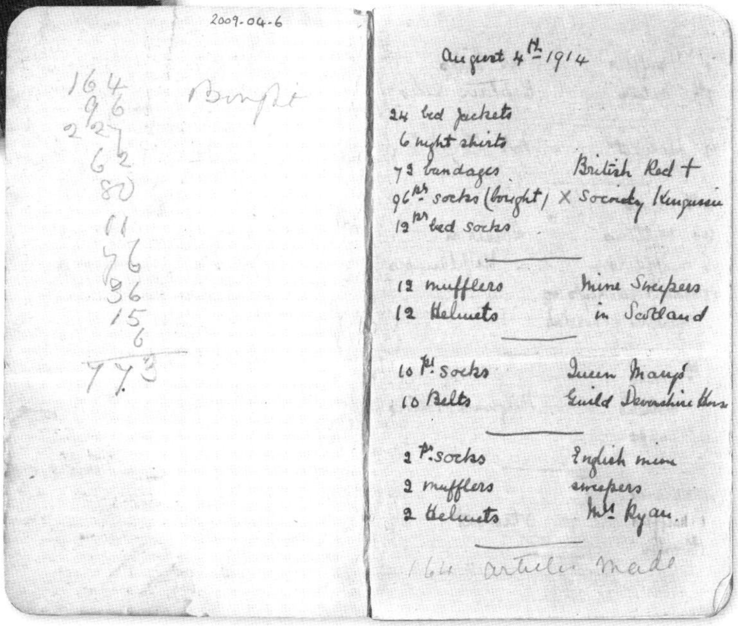

2009·04·6

164
9 6
2 2
6 2
80
11
7 6
36
15
6
773

Bought

August 4th 1914

24 bed jackets
6 night shirts
7 3 bandages   British Red +
96 prs socks (bought) X Society Kingussie
19 pr bed socks

12 mufflers   Mine Sweepers
12 Helmets   in Scotland

10 P. socks   Queen Mary's
10 Belts   Guild Devonshire Hse

2 P. socks   English mine
2 mufflers   sweepers
2 Helmets   Mrs Ryan

164 articles made

KNITTING SOCKS FOR DADDY'S MEN

Patriotic Song

Words and Music by

JEAN MUNRO MULLOY
(Wife of Trooper Mulloy, of South African fame)

⑤

Anglo Canadian Music Publishers Association, Limited, Toronto, Canada

students formed dedicated groups, and knitting 'bees' the length and breadth of the country were employed in knitting solely for soldiers in France. For more experienced knitters, *The Delineator* magazine, one of the country's most popular women's titles, suggested the complicated task of knitting two socks at a time using their own special pattern.

Across no-man's-land, German soldiers needed warmth and comfort as much as any Allied soldier, and in their homeland the craze for knitting was no less pronounced, at least while wool supplies lasted. Writing about German women in *The Times* in November 1916, D. Thomas Curtin commented:

> At the beginning of the war the click of knitting needles was heard everywhere in Germany. Shop girls knitted while waiting for customers, women knitted in trams and trains, at theatres, in churches and of course, in the home. The knitting is ceasing now for the very practical reason that the military authorities have commandeered all the wool that got through our blockade for the clothing of the soldiery.

Publicity photographs of German schoolgirls sitting in neat rows in their classroom, obediently knitting in unison, were at odds with the promulgated image of barbaric Germany and were scenes that could be easily replicated around the world. Across the warring nations, and regardless of race, it seemed that knitting was a universal language.

'Knitting Socks for Daddy's Men', a patriotic song with words and music by Jean Munro Mulloy, wife of Canadian soldier Trooper Mulloy, who was blinded during the Boer War but went on to have a successful academic and political career.

Collar in the New Crochet Point Lace

THE new crochet point lace is very pretty, the needle-made "filling" giving a rich and fragile appearance to an extremely durable and fine kind of crochet. As the filling is merely a twisted kind of stitch worked with an ordinary sewing needle there is no difficulty in making this lace.

Any number of small motifs, generally round but sometimes assuming the form of leaves or flowers, can be used. In the collar illustrated all the motifs are round, and there are seven patterns including the tiny edging motif.

Commencing with the larger motif in the centre back, and using Manlove's No. 70

"Knitted Comforts for Men on Land and Sea"

Useful work for anxious fingers. Woollen Socks, Helmets, Scarfs, Mittens, Wristlets, Cardigans, etc., are all garments which will do grateful service.

Book of the best illustrated recipes, in a limited edition, sent free for 2½d. in stamps. Apply early to

J. & J. BALDWIN & Partners, Ltd., HALIFAX, Eng.

Makers of the famous

Beehive Knitting Wools

("WHITE HEATHER WHEELING" is the quality recommended for "Knitted Comforts for Men on Land and Sea.")

Military- and naval-themed advertisement for Beehive Knitting Wools from J. & J. Baldwin & Partners of Halifax recommending its wools for 'anxious fingers' and advising patriotic knitters to apply for their book of 'best illustrated recipes'.

3

KNITTING FOR EVERYONE

In February 1915, *The Times* reported that Dame Ellen Terry was recovering from a cataract operation. Though Britain's finest actress was recovering well, she was beset by profound irritation that the operation had interfered with her progress of knitting for soldiers. Other actresses took up knitting too – the popular Phyllis Dare was pictured in *The Sketch* magazine in June 1915 engrossed in her knitting, with an elegant bag to carry her knitting accoutrements hanging from her wrist.

Dame Ellen's commitment was reflected throughout society and across class boundaries. Knitting was open to one and all, and even those who might not be able to afford wool could be provided with some through charitable networks. Nor was knitting solely a feminine pursuit. Many men who were above enlistment age took to knitting: 'In Birmingham,' wrote *The Times*, 'men who used to make cycle spokes have turned their hands to knitting needles.' Furthermore, as a

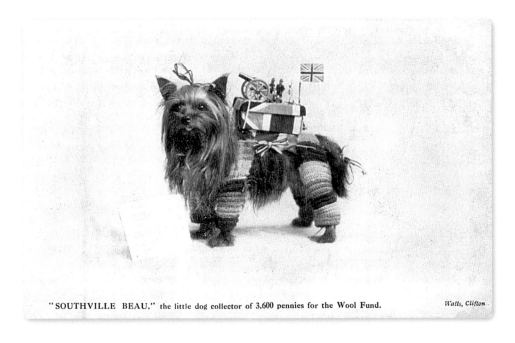

"SOUTHVILLE BEAU." the little dog collector of 3,600 pennies for the Wool Fund.

Watts, Clifton.

pastime, it provided convalescent soldiers and prisoners of war with something constructive to do. One British prisoner of war in Germany expressed his desire for a decent pair of needles, writing, 'I find my knitting a good hobby, but I want good needles. I have only pieces of wire now.' At the Interneerings Depot at Groningen, Holland, Commodore Wilfred Henderson described how the men were kept occupied knitting warm garments and, at the famous Netley military hospital in Hampshire, wounded men were also put to work knitting. It was also observed that recovering Canadian soldiers at Cliveden in Buckinghamshire had become deft with needles and yarn too.

Left: Even animals could help with the knitting effort. Southville Beau, a Yorkshire terrier, featured on a wartime postcard with news that he had collected 3,000 pennies for the Wool Fund to knit socks and balaclava helmets for the boys in the trenches.

Right: Advertisement for Baldwin's Ladyship Wools brand, recommending its 'softness and springiness ... warmth without weight'.

THE DESIRE TO HELP

Things Every Woman Can Do.

KNITTED COMFORTS FOR OUR MEN

In this great work of providing our soldiers with woollen comforts, it is the first duty of each lady to get Wools that will be suitable for the purpose.

Remember that the men have to march day after day, and then think of the discomfort or pain that they would suffer if wearing socks made of hard, coarse wools, or socks with holes in them.

"LADYSHIP" WOOLS

"Sports"
"Primrose Petticoat"
&"X Fingering"

have that softness and springiness that is necessary, and are the most durable of all wools.

The special quality of the wool gives warmth without weight, durability without hardness.

Primrose Petticoat and **Ladyship Sports Wool** for mufflers, caps, helmets, body bands, mittens, sleeping socks and sweater coats.

Ladyship "X" Fingering for socks, gloves, coats and vests.

Ladyship Leaflets No. 18, 19 and 20, give complete and simple directions for all kinds of Soldiers' Comforts, price $1\frac{1}{2}$d. each post free, 4d. post free for the set.

The Ladyship Wools can be bought at all the leading wool shops.

If any difficulty in obtaining them send a post card to the manufacturers.

BALDWIN & WALKER, LTD.
HALIFAX.

The requirement for comforts also opened up employment opportunities for the needy at home. The Economic Relief Committee inaugurated a knitting factory in Islington, which had the dual benefit of producing yet more comforts for troops as well as providing employment for women from the Labour Exchange; the Belgian refugees who had flooded into Britain in 1914 were also a useful source of manpower in this respect. In Cheshire, Sale Hall was occupied by twelve

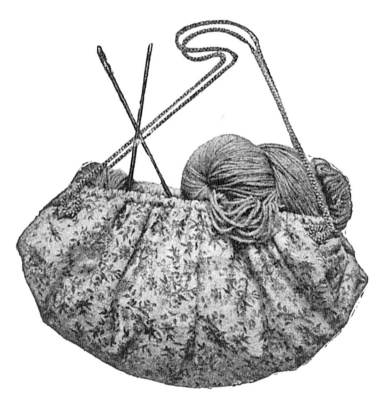

A boat-shaped knitting bag in colour-printed shantung silk lined with cotton, available from Liberty at a cost of 9s 11d. Just the ticket for enthusiastic knitters who liked to travel with their equipment.

Queen Alexandra's Field Force Fund was one of several organisations that encouraged donations of knitted garments and ensured their delivery to the front. This card indicates three cases of comforts sent to the 7th Prince of Wales's (North Staffordshire) Regiment in Gallipoli in November 1915.

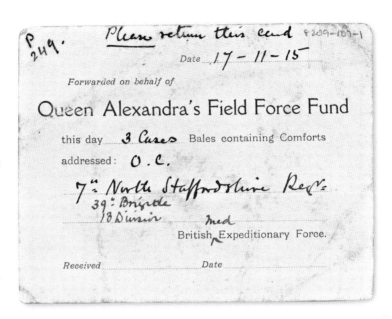

Belgian refugee families, amounting to fifty-one individuals. The *Manchester Guardian*, reporting on this little community, noted that, 'In the evening, when the children are in bed, and the talk dwells on the war and the desolated towns, the women take to knitting socks and comforters for the soldiers. They would be grateful for large gifts of wool.' At a workhouse in Poland Street in London, Jewish women refugees also spent much of their time knitting socks.

One young knitter, a girl of only seven, tragically paid the ultimate price for her devotion to the cause according to one newspaper report. While absorbed in her knitting at Colchester, she walked into the path of a military motor lorry and was killed.

"WHAT WOMEN ARE DOING"—OUR ANSWER TO THE "DAILY MAIL"

Society at work. Illustration by Annie Fish, to accompany the 'Letters of Eve' column in *The Tatler* magazine, showing a group of society ladies sewing and knitting for the troops.

Left: International movie star and 'America's Sweetheart' Mary Pickford pictured on a film set knitting for the Red Cross.

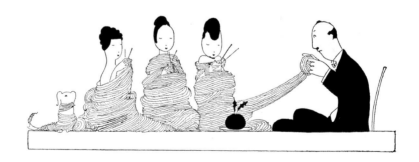

Three ladies knee-deep in khaki wool knit furiously and engage the help of a civilian male to wind their yarn. Illustration by Annie Fish in *The Tatler*, 23 December 1914.

The popular actress Phyllis Dare (1890–1975) pictured in *The Sketch* magazine in June 1915 engrossed in her knitting, with a special bag to carry her needles and wool hanging from her wrist.

Across the country, people devised enterprising ways to use knitting to boost funds for war charities. In Byfleet, 240 laundry girls combined to knit a scarf for Prince Albert (the future King George VI). Each girl paid 1s to knit one row and the £12, along with the scarf, was sent to Queen Mary, who presented the money to the Royal Navy Prisoners of War Fund. The scarf was presented to Prince Albert, who perhaps wore it with pride while a midshipman on board HMS *Collingwood*.

In 1917, a film was distributed aimed at educating the public about the work connected with the provision of comforts for men at the front. Opening with scenes in the offices of Sir Edward Ward where requests for goods were received, it went on to show a class of young schoolgirls who, wrote the *Manchester Guardian*, were 'knitting mufflers and socks with an industry that seems quite undisturbed by the presence of the camera man ...' West End shop assistants were shown making bandages in a London hospital supply workroom, while women munition workers were pictured spending their precious leisure time knitting. Scenes of packing and shipping followed before the end scenes showed parcels being delivered at a casualty station and base hospital, where 'the joy with which they are received is very evident'.

Girls from the cast of 'The Country Girl' at Daly's Theatre in
November 1914 posing for a publicity photograph during a break in
rehearsals, with their knitting needles poised as they knit mittens
and mufflers for soldiers.

Right: Countess Zia Torby (later Lady Zia Wernher) and her sister
Countess Nada Torby (later Mountbatten), daughters of Grand
Duke Michael and prominent figures in society, organising a group
of society ladies who are busily engaged in packing knitted gloves
and mittens for soldiers as part of the war effort in October 1914.

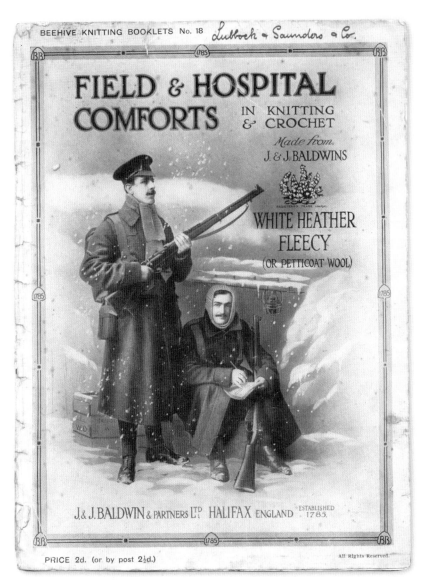

Baldwin's produced a series of knitting booklets. This one features a rather picturesque scene of British soldiers warmly wrapped up against the cold in a snowy trench.

'Sister Susie's Sewing Shirts for Soldiers', composed by Hermann Darewski, with lyrics by R.P. Weston, was popularised by Al Jolson during the war. In this postcard by Agnes Richardson, Susie turns her hand to knitting.

EVERYBODY'S DOING IT

To keep our Tommies warm . . . .

"Sister Susie."

Active Service

'Active Service'
postcard by
Harold Copping
around 1915.

Absent_yet Near.

I wish I were near to tell you,
How deep in my thoughts you dwell,
But though we're parted to-day dear,
This card will my kind greetings tell.

'Absent – yet Near.' Postcards offered the opportunity for sentimentality as well as humour and many showed images of parted husbands, wives and sweethearts. Here, a soldier's wife at home presents a picture of womanly domesticity – and she is, of course, knitting.

The need for warmth and protection from the elements is reflected in this advertisement for Debenham & Freebody from *The Illustrated War News* in December 1914, featuring items such as fur-lined coats and waistcoats and sleeping bags.

The Man in Khaki knitting kit, designed to make the knitting of socks for troops as simple and efficient as possible. The box, featuring an officer in uniform with a helmet, contained instructions, diagrams and a tape measure.

Every Woman Can help

Night and day the "Boys" require the ministry of women—and every woman, whatever her calling, can help. Socks, Belts, Mittens, Mufflers, Jerseys, Helmets, etc., with Paton's Alloa Knitting Wools, there is nothing easier to make. Paton's Wools are easy to knit, soft to the touch, durable and comfortable in wear.

PATON'S
ALLOA KNITTING WOOLS

Made in Khaki, Navy, Natural Grey, Drab, and in all requisite colours. Paton's Wools are entirely British.

Useful Guide on "How to Knit Soldiers' and Sailors' Comforts," for 1½d. in stamps, postage free.

Nearest retailer's Address, who will send free patterns, will be forwarded on application to
PATON'S, ALLOA, SCOTLAND, or to
192 ALDERSGATE STREET, LONDON, E.C. 1.

Printed for the Proprietors by ED. & CHAS. STRAKER, Ltd., 12-13 St. John's Square, London, E.C. 1.
Sole Agents for the Colonies—GORDON & GOTCH, Ltd., London, Australia, Canada, etc.
Sole Agents for South Africa—THE CENTRAL NEWS AGENCY, Ltd.
Wholesale Trade Agents—E. MARLBOROUGH & Co., 51 Old Bailey, London, E.C. 4.
Rates and Terms for Advertisements upon application.

'Every Woman Can Help': Paton's advertisement featuring a Red Cross nurse spending her spare time productively.

Leaflet issued by Farmer & Company of Sydney, Australia, instructing knitters on how to knit two socks at the same time on a single set of knitting needles. This ingenious technique was undertaken by a number of experienced knitters in order to increase production.

A Revolution
in
Sock Knitting

How to Knit Two Socks at the one time
on a single set of knitting needles.

PRICE 1/-

Issued by FARMER & COMPANY LIMITED, Sydney.
Half proceeds to be donated to 55th Battalion Comforts Fund.

BEEHIVE KNITTING BOOKLETS No. 17.

Knitted
COMFORTS FOR MEN
on LAND and SEA

Made from
J. J. BALDWINS

TRADE MARK

"WHITE HEATHER"
SPECIALITIES

J. & J. BALDWIN & PARTNERS LTD. HALIFAX ENGLAND ESTD. 1785

PRICE 2d. (or by post 2½d.)

All Rights Reserved.

This particular booklet from J. & J. Baldwin features a soldier, sailor and merchant seaman conversing together on its cover – perhaps discussing their urgent need for the women of Britain to knit them more socks.

Right: 'Knitting Song': American music sheet cover.

KNITTING

SONG

WRITTEN AND COMPOSED BY
MURIEL BRUCE

CHAPPELL & CO. LTD.
41 EAST 34th ST.   347 YONGE STREET
NEW YORK   TORONTO
LONDON   *All Rights Reserved*   MELBOURNE

AND
BARON ALIOTTI

PRICE 60¢

"Women's" Weapons

Compliments of

C. T. SHERER COMPANY

Worcester, Mass.

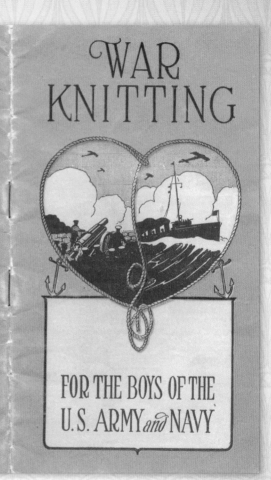

WAR KNITTING

FOR THE BOYS OF THE U.S. ARMY and NAVY

Front and back covers of an elegantly designed knitting booklet from the C.T. Sherer Company of Massachussetts. Note the term 'Women's Weapons', referring to knitting needles and yarn.

"EVERYBODY CAN HELP."

DRAWN BY E. BLAMPIED.

'Everybody can help' by Edmund Blampied, published in *The Sketch* on 9 December 1914. Two rather effeminate young men, obviously not cut out to be soldiers, instead help the war effort by knitting for the troops and smoking – another popular wartime activity.

From the painting by Gabriel Nicolet in the possession of Messrs Allen & Hanburys, Ltd

ALLEN &
HANBURYS, L.TD
LONDON

'Allenburys' Diet
for Invalids

PARIS · DURBAN
SYDNEY · TORONTO
SHANGHAI

Advertisement for 'Allenbury's' Diet for Invalids, featuring a painting by the artist Gabriel Nicolet showing a pristine nurse busy knitting by a patient's bedside.

"DARN IT!"

Darning socks – an example of wartime economy rendered in the elegant, fluid style of the artist Edmund Blampied. From *The Tatler*, 19 January 1916.

HER EXCELLENCY'S KNITTING BOOK

For the Empire and for Freedom
We all must do our bit ;
The men go forth to battle,
The women wait—and knit.

Annette Liverpool

Front cover of *Her Excellency's Knitting Book*, published in 1915 by Annette Foljambe, Countess of Liverpool, wife of the Governor of New Zealand. New Zealand held a 'Sock Day' in May of the same year. The poem on the cover reflects traditionally accepted gender roles.

Right: The First World War knitting phenomenon even spread to the stage. 'The Knitting Club Meets' was a light-hearted play following a group of American knitters and their witty banter during group meetings.

No Plays Exchanged

BAKER'S EDITION OF PLAYS

The Knitting Club Meets

Price, 25 Cents

WA... ...MPANY

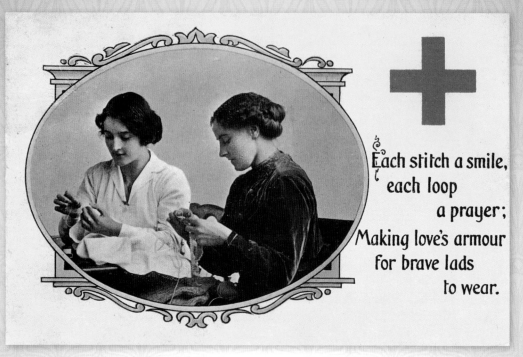

Each stitch a smile,
each loop
a prayer;
Making love's armour
for brave lads
to wear.

Women working industriously at their knitting was a frequent subject for patriotic postcards – as were sentimental rhymes.

Right: 'Story of the Knitted Scarf', published in *The Tatler* on 22 December 1915. An enterprising soldier, having received an enormous scarf knitted by a kindly mother or aunt back at home, converts it into a comfortable hammock across his trench.

MAKING

RECEIVING

ALTERING

USING

"I wish you'd get on with your knitting."

One of a series of wartime postcards featuring cute, chubby-faced children, with the popular motif of a soldier resignedly press-ganged into winding wool by his sweetheart.

E', I'm that tired out—I've been knitting socks for soldiers every bit o' this day!

Delightful Bamforth postcard showing a lady worn out from knitting socks for soldiers. Unfortunately, she has been so busy she has neglected to attend to her own stockings.

"I do hope they'll fit!"

Postcard by H.G.C. Marsh Lambert showing a small girl presenting a pair of misshapen, hand-knitted khaki socks to a soldier and expressing the hope that they fit. He doesn't look convinced.

The twin preoccupations of soldiers in kilts and knitting add up to a rather cheeky joke in this postcard illustrated by Fred Spurgin and postmarked 1916.

NAUGHTY NETTA'S KNITTING KNICKERS
FOR THE SEAT OF WAR.
Chacun doit se rendre utile.

"WE MUST ALL DO SOMETHING FOR OUR COUNTRY!"

A popular and patriotic postcard from the period.

'England expects that every woman this day will do her duty' – one of Mabel Lucie Attwell's cute, chubby-cheeked children demonstrates a determined patriotism as she knits an enormous khaki sock in this postcard produced by the Carlton Publishing Company around 1915.

England expects that every woman this day will do her duty.

NUMBER 5

2ᴰ   2ᴰ

The Needle Worker.

MARCH, 1915

CONTENTS.

A BELGIAN KÉPI

MONTHLY MAGAZINE
for everyone interested in
THE ART & CRAFT OF THE NEEDLE.

KNITTING COMPETITION FOR MEN AND BOYS

Front cover of *The Needleworker* from March 1915 featuring a knitted version of the Belgian 'képi' cap.

Music sheet contrasting the peaceful industry of the knitting woman with a scene of war on the Western Front: both the woman at home and the soldier abroad doing their duty.

EVERY GIRL IS KNITTING

FOR SOME MOTHER'S SON IN FRANCE

Featured and Written by
HAWLEY AND **BELLAIRE**
IN SUPREME VAUDEVILLE

5

JEFF BRANEN
PUBLISHER
145 W. 45TH ST. N.Y.

THE CUMBERLAND MITTEN.
Specially Designed for the Use of Soldiers at the Front.

[In following instructions are for knitted mittens, which have been arrived at after several experiments. The mittens when submitted to soldiers who had seen many

number of these mittens were made last winter and sent out to the trenches, and have met with the highest praise.

No. 1 illustration shows the mitten as worn when freedom is desired for the fingers and thumb, and No. 2 with the mitten drawn down over the thumb and fingers, giving greater warmth when freedom is not necessary. One point let me impress upon my readers, namely, when the mittens have been completed, turn back the portions as shown in illustration No. 1, and tack the pair together at the thumb, the fingers, and at the wrist, so that when a soldier receives them he may at once see how they are to be worn. Of his own initiative he will turn them down as in illustration No. 2 when the occasion requires. Also, and let this be writ large in a knitter's memory, tack them together with white cotton, not wool, or the soldier will be likely to cut the mitten as the tacking—and let this be done securely.

This mitten has the further advantage of being easily soiled. I knit the hand portion in khaki, and, as this colour is more difficult to procure than others, I make the hand for portion in any other colour providing it is stable.

Instructions.—Cast on 56 loops. Knit 28 ribs. Knit 18 loops, and then cast on 10 loops for the thumb on the needle upon which you have just knitted the 18. Knit back to the wrist, but do not knit the last loop. Knit to

the end of the 10 loops. Then knit back to the wrist, leaving 2 loops unknitted. Then knit to the end of the 10 loops, then back to the wrist, leaving 3 loops. Repeat until you have 10 unknitted loops. Now knit up the remaining 18 loops (these 18 loops are on the short needle in No. 3 illustration). Then knit 11 ribs, or more should a wider mitten be desired.

Sew up the thumb and the hand portion of the mitten. Then take up 44 loops at the wrist, and knit 2 and purl 2 for about 4 inches.

Needles, 10 bell gauge. Wool, Alloa.

AUGUSTA A. VARTY-SMITH.

THE MANY GOOD POINTS OF THE COCKATOO KNITTING AND OTHER WOOLS.

An excellent and very comprehensive set of patterns of knitting and rug wools reaches us from those well-known manufacturers, the Cockatoo Company, Burley-in-Wharfe-

MENUS FOR EVERY DAY OF THE YEAR. With over 800 recipes. By M. Jebb Scott. In this useful book the menus are arranged chronologically, a page being devoted to each day, and comprise breakfast, luncheon, dinner, and servants' dinner. Following this are over 800 recipes of certain special dishes included in the menus. The book is not intended to compete with the cookery books which have been published for use in large establishments or hotels, but is for households wherein variety must be combined with economy, and, among other things, it aims at preventing waste by using food which might otherwise be useless. Price 5s. net.—FIELD & QUEEN (HORACE COX) LTD., Windsor House, Bream's Buildings, London, E.C.—[ADVT.]

with Alsace bow of wide ribbon to match in lieu of a cap, a tiny bow of the same finishing the neck of the orthodox black afternoon dress. Little muslin collars and cuffs are then all that is needed, and these, anyway, make to laundry demands, even if maids will not don them themselves. Heliotrope and grey both look very well for the aprons, as does the curious blue which is neither mauvy nor royal nor nattier, but a blend of all three, the blue—or an imitation of it!—which Romney loved to paint. For the benefit of those who have never dabbled in the practical side of things, mercerised lawn may be mentioned as admirable for the aprons; it runs a wide width and in particularly pretty colours, is of charmingly fine, silky appearance, and even in these days costs only 1s. 6d. or thereabouts at the most a yard. The aprons in mind are made quite plain, with deep hems and broad double borders stitched on at the

sides continued in shoulder straps from the square bibs, and are more or less the size of the little spotted muslin ones now so much in vogue. Three yards and a half of the lawn easily makes four of these, so that they work out at little more than a shilling each. Of course, where good fitting uniform black dresses are not available they could be larger, though then they would probably need ironing oftener; for with the dark colour an iron freshens up the apron with very occasional washing.

Then, for the mornings, of course one falls back on overalls—we are an overalled nation in these days! The ordinary garment, however, does not appeal for the purpose. But have it—of grey gingham, for instance—made with a plastron front running from shoulder to hem slightly shaped to the waist, with a band each side to button at the back tightly and so hold the fullness at the back really in place, with a square yoke across the shoulders at the back into which the fullness of the lower part is gathered; bishop sleeves to the wrist; and a plain collar band to which a little turn-over muslin collar can be tacked, and the effect is quite different. Black Alsace bows in place of caps and black bows to finish off the neck in front give quite a smart effect, and this is half the battle with mistress and maid alike. Of course, we may—should—regret the fresh prettiness of the washing dresses and aprons. But it would be a war measure purely, and any way preferable to any half measures where the now generally accepted uniform is concerned. Moreover, the example would not be without its value. L.

I WONDER WHO'S KNITTING FOR ME ?

WORDS BY
RAYMOND LEVEEN
MUSIC BY
JESSE WINNE

5

WINLEE MUSIC CO.
145 West 45th Street.
NEW YORK

Left: 'I Wonder Who's Knitting For Me?' An American soldier's daydream consists of imagining the girls back at home knitting for his comfort.

A rather handsome young man modelling a knitted helmet with extended 'cape' featured on the cover of an American Red Cross leaflet.

ARC 400
September 10, 1917

THE AMERICAN RED CROSS
WOMAN'S BUREAU
WASHINGTON, D. C.

Instructions *for* Knitting

Sweaters, Mufflers, Helmets, Socks,
Wristlets, Wash-cloths, Bottle-covers

Muffler

MUFFLER

2 hanks of yarn (½ lb.); 1 pair Red Cross Needles No. 3. Cast on 50 stitches or 11 inches. Plain knitting for 68 inches.

A generous muffler made to a pattern found in an American Red Cross leaflet.

Be Useful in Time of War

Weldon's 2d.

GARMENTS AND HOSPITAL

COMFORTS

for our

Soldiers and Sailors

Plain Knitted Sock.

Knitted Sleeping Helmet.

HOW TO CUT OUT AND MAKE

DAY SHIRT	NIGHTSHIRT (Open at Back)
NIGHTSHIRT	
PYJAMA SUIT	NIGHTSHIRT (Open Back & Front)
DRESSING GOWN	
UNDERVEST	FLANNEL BELT
BED-JACKET	NIGHTINGALE
NURSE'S APRON	AND SLEEVES
SURGEON'S OVERALL	

PAPER PATTERNS of the Garments 4½d. each.

HOW TO KNIT

BALACLAVA HELMET	SLEEPING CAPS
	SWEATER
MITTENS	PLAIN SOCKS
BELT	CARDIGAN
NECK SCARFS	JACKET
BED SOCKS	KNEECAPS, Etc.

HOW TO CROCHET

SLEEPING CAPS AND SCARFS
D'OYLEYS TO PROTECT LIQUID
FROM DUST AND FLIES

HOW TO MAKE
FLANNEL BALACLAVA HELMET,
FLANNEL CRIMEAN SLEEPING CAP,
COVER FOR HOT WATER BOTTLE,
BANDAGES, INVALID'S SLIPPERS, Etc.

A SECOND SERIES of Garments and Hospital Comforts now ready, price Twopence.

'Be Useful in Time of War.' Front cover of 'Weldon's Garments and Hospital Comforts for our Soldiers and Sailors'.

KNITTED WRISTLETS
With Thumbhole

MATERIALS—
½ hank **Sunlight** Knitting Worsted, 2 No. 10 Steel Needles.

Cast on 52 stitches. Knit 2, purl 2 for 12 inches. Sew up, leaving slit for thumb 2 inches long, 4 inches from one end. This should be 6 inches wide before joining.

KNITTED HELMET

MATERIALS—1 hank **Sunlight** Knitting Worsted, 2 No. 4 Knitting Needles, 4 No. 10 Steel Knitting Needles.

With No. 4 needles cast on 54 stitches, knit plain 10 inches for front; slip off on spare needle. Work another piece to correspond, 5 inches for back.

Slip the stitches of both pieces onto 3 steel needles, having 36 stitches on each needle; knit 2, purl 2 for 5 inches; bind off 30 stitches very loosely to make the opening for the face; knit 2, purl 2, forward and backward, for 13 rows.

Cast on 30 stitches *loosely*, and on 3 needles knit 2, purl 2 for 2½ inches. Knit one round plain; then narrow by

knitting the last 2 stitches on each needle together, every row, until there are 8 stitches left on each needle; then knit 2 stitches together all around, leaving 4 stitches on each needle; then draw loop of the yarn through all 12 stitches with a crochet hook, and fasten firmly. Knit rather snugly.

KNITTED SCARF

MATERIALS—2 hanks **Sunlight** Knitting Worsted, 2 No. 5 Knitting Needles.

Cast on 50 stitches. Knit plain until 58 inches long. This should measure 10 inches in width.

DON'TS FOR THE KNITTERS OF SOCKS

Don't cast on tightly. An otherwise well knitted sock may become useless by this tight cord at the top.

Don't knot your wool. Join it by splicing the ends or leave two or three inches of each end and darn back carefully.

Don't forget that a man may not have a chance to change his socks for many days, and a lump or knot brings a blister. If the blister breaks, blood poisoning may result in the loss of a foot or even a life. We cannot afford to lose our men through negligence or ignorance.

Don't make a heel with a seam.

Don't use needles too fine for the wool. The knitting should be elastic; if too tightly knitted the sock becomes hard and boardlike in use.

Don't make a foot less than 11 inches long.

When a size smaller needle is used add 8 stitches to directions given.

Always measure with a rule.

Sunlight YARNS

4

KNITTING FUN

As the national mania for knitting gained pace in the first few months of the war, it was inevitable that the subject, ripe with comic opportunity, would become part of popular culture.

Of the millions of postcards that zipped back and forth across the Channel, many of them took knitting as their theme, with rousing captions such as 'We all must do something for our country' or 'Every woman must do her duty', ensuring that even the most light-hearted missive reminded everyone of their patriotic obligation. From the humorous to the romantic, postcard artists pictured chubby-cheeked children, hopeful sweethearts and comfortable-looking grandmothers all 'knitting their bit'. While some were sentimental, others could be quite ribald, such as one card by Fred Spurgin – 'Naughty Netta's Knitting Knickers for the Seat of War', a play on the old joke about what a Scotsman wears under his kilt. One of the most popular songs from the period, 'Sister Susie's Sewing Shirts

Few body parts were left uncovered by woolly comforts: patterns for wristlets, helmets and scarves featured in a booklet issued by Sunlight Yarns.

for Soldiers', recorded by Al Jolson, among others, was the subject of another postcard by Agnes Richardson, who depicted a young flapper with a sweet expression and her knitting needles poised.

Numerous songs and poems on the theme of knitting were published, including a number by the popular writer Jessie Pope, whose poems were published in the *Daily Mail, Punch* and other national publications. Songs about knitting proliferated, particularly in the United States, with sentimental titles such as 'Every Girl is Knitting for Some Mother's Son in France' or 'Soldier, Soldier, Dear Unknown'. Knitting featured in the theatre, too, both on stage – often in war-themed revues such as 'Business as Usual' at the Hippodrome – as well as off stage. In November 1914, the female cast of 'The Country Girl', playing at Daly's Theatre in Leicester Square, London, posed for a publicity photograph during rehearsals, arranged artfully atop and around a hay cart, each of them happily engaged in knitting. It was the sort of photograph that would have warmed the cockles of the heart of any serving soldier.

Knitting even made it onto the stage. In America, a short play entitled 'The Knitting Club Meets' published by Baker's focused entirely on a female knitting group, the members of which all owned capacious knitting bags and grumbled about the monotony of using khaki wool. One character, Eleanor, even argues a case for cladding the troops in pastel hues:

Humph! The government hadn't tried wearing nothing but khaki when it made that rule, I'm sure. The men's

The popular nursery rhyme given a woolly wartime twist in this postcard drawn by Ridgewell from 1916.

socks and sweaters are always underneath – can't possibly be seen from a distance – so why shouldn't they be a cheerful pink or blue instead of that dreadful, bilious no-color?

She had a point.

The national enthusiasm for knitting did not escape the pen of cartoonists in magazines such as *Punch, The Tatler* and *The Sketch* either. Who could resist gently mocking the tangled scrapes suffered by knitting novices, or envisaging the expression of recipients when oddly sized and shaped items arrived in the trenches sent by well-meaning knitters at home? One cartoon shows a soldier unravelling one poorly made sock, murmuring 'She loves me, she loves me not', while another contrives to convert a gargantuan muffler into a comfy hammock. In *Punch*, one tenacious little girl sits wrestling with her needles and yarn and exclaims, 'Mother, dear! I do hope this war won't be over before I finish my sock!' The cartoon was published in September 1914 when many assumed the war would 'be over by Christmas', unaware of the four more long years of knitting ahead.

Soldiers themselves, faced with comforts of varying quality, could barely resist gently mocking the attempts of their overseas benefactors. One letter from a New Zealand infantryman to Audrey J. Reid contained a particularly cheeky but irresistible rhyme:

'Mother, dear! I do hope this war won't be over before I finish my sock!' A little girl gets to grips with needles and wool in an attempt to do her bit. Illustration by G. Jennis in *Punch*, 30 September 1914.

Mabel. "MOTHER, DEAR! I DO HOPE THIS WAR WON'T BE OVER BEFORE I FINISH MY SOCK!"

Life of a pair of socks
They are some fit!
I used one for a helmet
And the other for a mitt
Glad to hear
You're doing your bit –
But who the _____
Said you can knit?!

Right: H.F.C.
Skinner's
illustration
in *Punch,*
25 November
1914, of a British
soldier who, on
receiving a pair
of badly made
socks from
a sweetheart
in England,
proceeds to
unravel the yarn.

Left: Richard
Brook's
illustration
in *Punch* on
1 December
1915 showing
a biddable
gentleman being
disturbed from
his armchair
nap and used by
two ladies of the
house to wind
wool.

The Sentimentalist (who has received socks from England). "SHE LOVES ME; SHE LOVES ME NOT."

"GRANNY, I *AM* GLAD WE'VE LIVED TO SEE PEACE!"

Punch cartoon by Claude Shepperson, 18 December 1918, showing a little girl expressing her relief at surviving the war. It did rather go on longer than anyone expected! Granny smiles beatifically and carries on with her knitting.

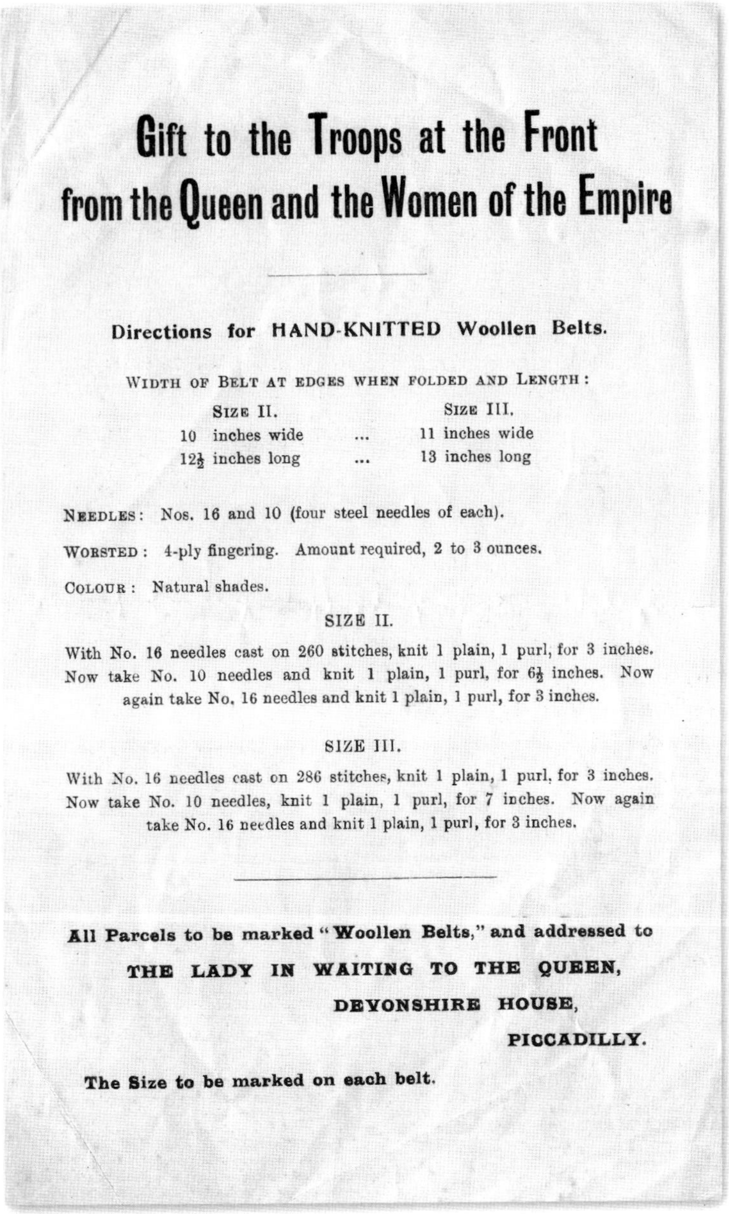

Gift to the Troops at the Front
from the Queen and the Women of the Empire

Directions for HAND-KNITTED Woollen Belts.

WIDTH OF BELT AT EDGES WHEN FOLDED AND LENGTH:

SIZE II.		SIZE III.
10 inches wide	...	11 inches wide
12½ inches long	...	13 inches long

NEEDLES: Nos. 16 and 10 (four steel needles of each).

WORSTED: 4-ply fingering. Amount required, 2 to 3 ounces.

COLOUR: Natural shades.

SIZE II.

With No. 16 needles cast on 260 stitches, knit 1 plain, 1 purl, for 3 inches. Now take No. 10 needles and knit 1 plain, 1 purl, for 6½ inches. Now again take No. 16 needles and knit 1 plain, 1 purl, for 3 inches.

SIZE III.

With No. 16 needles cast on 286 stitches, knit 1 plain, 1 purl, for 3 inches. Now take No. 10 needles, knit 1 plain, 1 purl, for 7 inches. Now again take No. 16 needles and knit 1 plain, 1 purl, for 3 inches.

All Parcels to be marked "Woollen Belts," and addressed to

THE LADY IN WAITING TO THE QUEEN,

DEVONSHIRE HOUSE,

PICCADILLY.

The Size to be marked on each belt.

Even royalty took an interest in knitting. This leaflet gives instructions for knitting woollen belts, which could then be sent to the Lady in Waiting to Queen Mary at Devonshire House where they would be collected and from there sent to the soldiers at the front.

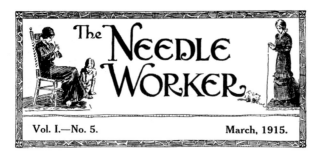

The NEEDLE WORKER

Vol. I.—No. 5.   March, 1915.

Knitting for Men and Boys

WE are pleased to find that our efforts to promote the art of knitting amongst men and boys are meeting with some considerable encouragement, and so we give another Competition for them.

A first prize of half a guinea will be given for the best pair of Baby's Gloves from instructions on page 87, and a similar prize for the best pair of mittens from instructions on page 84.

There will be other smaller prizes.

The Competition will close on the 10th of April, by which date all entries must reach the office of THE NEEDLE-WORKER, Cromwell House, High Holborn, W.C.

There is no age limit, but each competitor must state age and occupation to assist the judges in their decisions.

Articles will not be returned but will be sent to our noble defenders or their children.

The Knitting Song

(We acknowledge our obligation to Miss Jessie Pope for permitting us to reprint " The Knitting Song.")

Soldier lad, on the sodden ground,
  Sailor lad, on the seas,
Can't you hear a little clicketty sound
  Stealing across on the breeze ?
It's the knitting needles singing their song,
  As they twine the khaki or blue,
Thousands and thousands and thousands strong,
  Tommy and Jack, for you.

      Click—click—click !
      How they dart and flick,
    Flashing in the firelight to and fro !
      Now for purl and plain,
      Round and round again,
    Knitting love and luck in every row.

The busy hands may be rough or white,
  The fingers gouty or slim,
The careful eyes may be youthfully bright,
  Or they may be weary and dim.
Lady and workgirl, young and old,
  They've all got one end in view,
Knitting warm comforts against the cold,
  Tommy and Jack, for you.

      Click—click—click !
      How they dart and flick,
    Flashing in the firelight to and fro !
      Now for purl and plain,
      Round and round again,
    Knitting love and luck in every row.

Knitting away by the midnight oil,
  Knitting when day begins ;
Lads, in the stress of your splendid toil
  Can't you hear the song of the pins ?
Clicketty click—through the wind and the foam,
  It's telling the boys over there
That every " woolly " that comes from home
  Brings a smile and a hope and a prayer.

      Click—click—click !
      How they dart and flick,
    Flashing in the firelight to and fro
      Now for purl and plain,
      Round and round again,
    Knitting love and luck in every row.

                    JESSIE POPE.

Page from *The Needleworker* featuring 'The Knitting Song', by Jessie Pope, one of a number of popular knitting-themed poems and songs.

Right: Scouts formed a valuable part of the country's war effort – and were certainly deserving of comforts.

2D.

LEACH'S

GARMENTS for BOY SCOUTS

A REGULATION SCOUT'S JERSEY
For Boys from Eleven Years.

THE WOLF-CUB'S JERSEY
For Boys from Eight Years.

A JERSEY FOR THE SEA SCOUT

A KNITTED HELMET
With Ear Flaps

WELL-FITTING KHAKI STOCKINGS

KNITTED MUFFLER AND CAP in one

SCARVES: Knitted and Crocheted

MITTENS the Boy Scout can Knit himself

HOW TO MAKE A PAIR OF SHORTS
Full Instructions with Diagrams

THE CONTENTS OF THIS BOOK ARE STRICTLY COPYRIGHT

No. 14   ALL ORIGINAL DESIGNS   L

Knitting on the stage – scene from the revue 'Business as Usual' at the Hippodrome in November 1914.

Right: 'Two plain, one purl' – cartoon by Stan Terry in *The Tatler*, 4 April 1917.

Shooting Glove and Mittens

Soldier's Shooting Glove

A glove our heroes are asking for, with thumb and first finger free.

Use khaki shade of white heather wheeling, 3-ply, and No. 12 knitting needles.

Cast on 70 stitches and k. 5 inches of 3 k., 2 p., then k. 2 tog. of the 3 k., and p. 2, k. 2 for 2 inches more, then k. plain, knitting the 2 purl stitches together, making 42 stitches for hand. If finer wool is used, omit purling 2 together and leave the 56 for hand. K. 4 or 5 rows, then commence gusset for thumb. K. to within last stitch of 3rd needle, lift up half of stitch immediately below last stitch, k. this lifted up half stitch, k. last stitch, k. 2 rounds, then k. to within 2 stitches from end of 3rd needle. Lift up half of stitch below this last stitch knitted, k. this, k. next, now lift up and k. half of stitch below last stitch, and k. last stitch. Increase this way every 3rd row until there are 16 stitches made, take these on to 2 separate needles, cast on 5 stitches, and k. thumb about an inch and a half long. Last 4 rows k. 2, p. 2, and cast off.

Lift up made stitches by thumb and k. hand an inch longer, then take 14 stitches for half of 1st finger. Centre 2 of these stitches should come directly over 1st increases for thumb, k. 1st finger an inch long, then k. 2, p. 2, and cast off. K. all other stitches for 10 or 12 rows, then k. 2 tog., 3rd stitch from end of each needle ; 3 rows are knitted between 1st and 2nd narrowings, 2 rows between next, then 1 row. Finish by narrowing every row until only 12 stitches remain ; these draw up with a needle and end of the wool.

Warm Mittens for Our Soldiers

Use 5-ply fingering and steel knitting needles No. 12.

Cast on 65 stitches, 20 on each of two needles and 25 on third needle, and knit 4 inches of 3 k., 2 p. ; then k 2 of the 3 k together once, k. around again, then each side of this 2 k. together, k. 2 together again, which makes 2 k., 2 p. three times. K. around again, then narrow the same way each, side of last narrowings until all 3 k. are 2 k. Knit on now until mitten measures 7 inches, then commence thumb.

On one needle, in knitting the 2 k., k. first of the two, then lift half of stitch immediately below that which is being knitted. Knit this lifted-up half, k. next stitch, p 2, and so on all round twice, taking care to k. the 3 stitches where one was made. Next increase, k. first of the 3 stitches, lift one directly below k. this, k. centre stitch.

Now lift half of stitch below third of these stitches, k. this, 2 p., and so on. Increase the same way every third row until there are 17 plain k. stitches here. Take these 17 stitches off on to a piece of wool, cast on 4 stitches to make an extra 2 k., 2 p. by thumb, and k. on another inch. Now divide for half fingers, thus :

Let last of these cast-on stitches be centre of 15 stitches for first finger for right hand. Cast on 3 k. plain about an inch, then k. 4 rows of 2 k., 2 p. Cast off. Take 15 stitches for centre finger (8 from back portion of mitten and 7 from palm part), lift up stitches cast on of first finger, cast on 3 at opposite side, k. 1 round ; then, on needle where stitches are cast on, narrow by knitting 2 together, to make 20 stitches. K. 1 round more than first finger, k. 2, p. 2 as before for 4 rows, and cast off.

Third Finger.—Take 14 stitches, lift from second finger, and cast on as before, and narrow each side, making 18 stitches for this finger, and lift up for small finger to make 15 stitches. Next lift up stitches left for thumb, narrow once, and k. 20 stitches, taking up the cast-on stitches made here. K. plain 1 inch, then 4 rows of 2 k., 2 p. Cast off.

These instructions could be followed for a glove, leaving out the 2 k., 2 p., and knitting each finger the desired length. To take off each finger, k. 2 together third stitch from end of each needle in each row until 6 stitches remain. These draw up neatly with a small darning needle, cutting wool off 4 or 5 inches from top of finger. Tread this in needle.

These mitts should fit closely, so as not to be cumbersome. Made from these directions, mitts will fit a hand of ordinary size (medium) ; for a very large hand cast on 5 more stitches, and have 1 more stitch in each finger-part and thumb.

For left-hand mitten, let first cast-on stitch be centre of the 15 stitches for first finger.

In first and third finger, 3 k., 3 p. must be made on inside part, 18 stitches, not working 2 k., 2 p. all round, and there will be a 3 k. on inside part of small finger. 1 k., 1 p. could be made instead if worker prefers.

Note.—Often in glove or mitten knitting an extra stitch is needed to be picked up at commencement of fingers. These may always be narrowed off on inside portion of finger. The same applies to thumb.

It is important in glove making to get the fingers long enough, and it is better from the point of view of wear to make them too long rather than too short. For an average man's hand the thumb from the junction of the first finger to the top should measure about 2¾ inches. The first finger 3 inches ; the second, 3½ inches ; the third, 3¼ inches ; and the fourth, 2½ inches. For larger sized gloves length of the fingers must be increased in proportion.

5

KNITTING PATTERNS

A page from *Woman's Own* knitting supplement, with a pattern for shooting gloves and mittens.

For anyone keen to embark on knitting for Tommy during the war, there was no shortage of ideas or instruction. Pamphlets or books dedicated to patterns for comforts were produced by yarn manufacturers, associations and charities, and simple patterns for much-needed items such as socks frequently appeared in the national and specialist press. In 1915, the *British Journal of Nursing* offered guidance on the dimensions of mufflers for the Army according to the Director General of Voluntary Organisations, Sir Edward Ward: 'each muffler should measure 58" x 10" and be made on two No. 7 needles, taking 10oz of fairly thick drab or khaki wool.' *The Graphic* newspaper published a diagram showing how mittens could be made from old socks and stockings, a method devised by Dr George C. Cathcart of Harley Street,

Sleeve, Body Belt, and Chest Protector

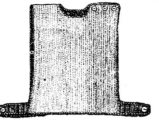

Chest Protector.

This chest-protector was knitted with white heather unshrinkable vest wool and No. 10 needles.

Cast on 80 stitches, and knit 1 row, purl back for 12 inches, then knit 30, cast off 20 stitches, knit next 30, turn, purl these last 30 stitches, turn, k. 1st 2 stitches together, knit next 28, turn, purl back, knit 1st 2 together, and repeat last 2 rows until there are 26 stitches on needle, knit these 26 stitches for 2½ inches for shoulder, then make a stitch beginning of each knitting row by knitting the 1st stitch 1st from front, then from back of stitch, until there are 30 stitches again on needle. Now leave this needle, and knit 2nd shoulder like 1st, knitting 2 together at end of knit row (by neck), and after 2½ inches are knitted of 26 stitches, make 1 at end of knit row by next, then there are 30 stitches on needle. Knit one row thus for buttonholes —k. 2, cast off 3, k. 9, cast off 3, k. 9, cast off 3, k. 1, turn, purl to end. Casting on 3 stitches over where 3 were cast off, next row cast off all. Next cast on 30 stitches, and knit forward, purl backward for 14 inches for back. At end here make 2 straps ; these may be either knitted or crocheted.

To Knit : Lift up stitches of last 12 rows, k. forward, p. backward until strap measures 5 or 6 inches, on one strap at end k. 5, cast off 3, k. 4, next row cast on 3 over casting off ; this is for a buttonhole. These straps may be knitted long enough to reach to front piece of protector, or pieces knitted each end of front and back, and buttoned across side ; this will keep the vest in place.

To Crochet : Lift up end stitch, and make double crochet up side in 12 stitches, turn with 1 ch. each row, and all through take up only the back stitch. The buttonhole is made in crochet by making 5 d.c., 3 ch., miss 3 d.c. below, 4 d.c. in next 4 d.c. These straps stretch, and are quite comfortable to wear. It is a good plan to work a row of d.c. all round the vest, as plain knitting is apt to curl up ; **1 row** of d.c. will prevent this. Vest takes only **4 ounces** of Baldwin's vest wool to make.

Comfortable Body Belt

Use white heather 4-ply petticoat fingering, and No. 10 needles.

Cast on 200 sts., and k. 1, p. 1 for 9 inches, then cast on 12 more stitches, and k. and p. backwards and forwards for about 3 inches This opening makes the belt easier to get on and off. In 2nd row before casting off, k. 1, p. 1, k 1. Cast off 4, k. and p. to end, and in returning cast on 3 stitches over, where 4 were cast off, and sew a flat linen button on flap made of 12 stitches.

Sleeve with Shaped Elbow

Use white heather petticoat fingering for sleeves, chest protectors, body belts, and all knitting where softness and elasticity is needed. This wool is beautifully soft, and 3 ounces will make a good size armlet. Use No. 10 knitting needles.

Cast on 72 stitches—24 on each of 3 needles. Knit 2 and purl 2 for 9 or 10 inches for wrist portion, then knit 3, purl 1 for 9 rounds. Now begin shaping for elbow ; knit 2 stitches of one of the 3, knit, turn, and work back, slip the 1st stitch ; purl next, knit

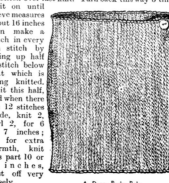

These knitted sleeves are so cosy for a wounded arm. Made loosely, they pass easily over bandages.

the purl stitch, purl 3, knit 1, purl 2. Turn, and slip the 1st stitch now. Knit 1, purl 1, knit 3, purl 1, knit 3, purl 1 for 4 rounds, then turn back and knit and purl as before, only commence in the 3 knit pass where the 1st turning back was done. Knit and purl again for 4 rounds, and then turn back from the next 3, knit pass last again, working each time to corresponding 3 knit at other side of turn back. Should a gap appear in next round, over where work was knitted back, lift half of stitch immediately below the next stitch that is to be knitted ; knit this lifted-up stitch, then knit next stitch, and pass lifted-up stitch over last knit. Turn back this way 5 times.

Knit on until sleeve measures about 16 inches then make a stitch in every 5th stitch by lifting up half of stitch below that which is being knitted. Knit this half, and when there are 12 stitches made, knit 2, purl 2, for 6 or 7 inches ; or for extra warmth, knit this part 10 or 12 inches, Cast off very loosely.

A Deep Body Belt.

who had supplied the London Scottish Regiment with the recycled items.

A number of patterns in this book were originally published in *The Queen* magazine. Launched in 1861 by Samuel Beeton (husband of the more famous Mrs Isabella Beeton), *The Queen* was aimed at a middle-class readership and covered domestic matters and society news as well as social welfare issues. The First World War found the magazine in its element, offering advice and guidance on a whole range of ways for women to help the war effort, from economising on food to training in first aid. Its needlework column, 'The Work Table', had been a feature of the magazine since its inception, and its wartime columns instructed readers on how to sew and knit articles for the needy, from clothing for Belgian refugee children to a whole gamut of knitted comforts for soldiers such as rifle gloves (leaving the thumb and forefinger free), knitted puttees, balaclavas with ear flaps or trench hose. Patterns appeared regularly throughout the four years of war. The first, in their 5 September issue, gave instructions for making a crocheted sock and a nurse's 'spencer' (a kind of cardigan), while as late as 16 November 1918, the magazine was still offering refined and improved knitting ideas, this time in the form of the Warleigh mitten, with gauntlets to prevent jacket cuffs from getting damp.

Other patterns are gleaned from original pamphlets from the period, produced by wool companies such as Weldon's or Baldwin's, as well as women's magazines like *Woman's Own* or leaflets produced by just one of the countless charities acting to provide comforts for soldiers and sailors abroad.

No area of the body was left unclad by Britain's knitters. This page from *Woman's Own* offers a chest protector, knitted sleeve and deep body belt for complete snugness.

'Recipes' for standard items such as knitted helmets or mittens proliferated, but it is interesting to note the small variations of detail from one item to the next. Sometimes, for instance, a helmet might have ear holes – essential if it were for a man working in communications – while others did not. Some balaclavas came with 'cape' extensions to warm the neck and chest, mittens and gloves were tailored to allow infantrymen to manipulate a rifle, while there was a myriad of specially designed constructions for protecting or supporting the wounds of men in hospital.

Whatever was needed, whether it was a smoking cap for a convalescent, an abdominal belt for keeping chills at bay, mittens for men on minesweepers or a sleeping helmet for nights spent out in the cold French winter, the nation's knitters provided it. Knitting for Tommy – and for Jack – was an essential element of the war effort. It kept the fighting forces warm, boosted morale among the men and gave a meaningful occupation to those who were desperate to do something to help.

Britain's knitters were anxious that the boys at the front would know they were not forgotten. Now it is our turn to remember them.

Invalid slipper and knitted kneecap from *Woman's Own*, 3 October 1914.

More Garments for the Soldiers and Sailors

Send your garments when finished to Stores Dept., British Red Cross Society, 83, Pall Mall, London, S.W., or to your local branch of the British Red Cross Society. A list of contents should be placed outside each parcel sent.

Quickly Worked Invalid's Slipper

Two and a half ounces of J. & J. Baldwin's 3-ply White Heather, Grey Wheeling, or a 4-ply Beehive Scotch Fingering. No. 10 hook. Work firmly throughout.

Commence with 7 ch., turn, miss the 1st chain, 1 d.c. into each of the next 5 ch., 3 d.c. into the 6th ch., then work down the *opposite* side of the ch., making 1 d.c. into each stitch. Turn. *Make 1 ch. to turn each row,* and be careful not to miss the 1st stitch in each row which is directly under the hook. Always pick up the back thread nearest forefinger.

2nd row : 1 d.c. into each stitch of previous row. Work forwards and backwards, making 3 d.c. into the centre stitch of *every other* row until there are 42 stitches in the row.

To make a firm edge, insert the hook through both threads when working the *last* stitch of each row.

Now commence the side. Work d.c. into d.c. on the first 11 stitches of the front, and continue working forwards and backwards (11 stitches) for 5 ridges, then increase 1 stitch at top edge in every 5th row until you have 14 stitches. Work 14 stitches to the row until the centre of the back is reached. The second half of the sides is worked to correspond, decreasing at the top edge to 11 stitches in the row. Join neatly to the front of slipper, and s.-s. on the right side of the work around the lower edge. With a coloured wool make 4 rows of s.-s. round the top edge. When working the s.-s. do not pull the loop upward as in d.c., but draw it towards you.

Fleecy soles can be purchased for a few pence, or ¼-inch-thick leather can be bought at a saddler's. Stand a man's slipper on a piece of felt or leather, pencil round, and cut to the pencil mark, sew a piece of flannel inside, and stitch with thick thread the crocheted slipper to the sole, putting the needle backwards and forwards closely, an eight of an inch from the edge of the material.

Knitted Kneecap

A pair of No. 8 bone knitting needles and 2 ounces of J. & J. Baldwin's Beehive Fingering 4-ply will be required for one pair

Cast on 48 stitches.

1st row : K. 1, p. 1 ; repeat to end of row.

Repeat the 1st row 19 times.

21st row : * k. 1, p. 1 ; repeat from * 10 times, k. 1 in the front and back of the next st., k. 2, k. 1 in front and back of next st., * k. 1, p. 1, repeat to end.

22nd row : * k. 1, p. 1, repeat from * 10 times, k. 6, * k. 1, p. 1, repeat to end.

23rd row : Same as 21st row, only k. 4, not 2.

24th row : * k. 1, p. 1, repeat 10 times, k. 8, * k. 1, p. 1, repeat to end.

Repeat the last 2 rows 3 times more, each time k. 2 more between the increasings, and in each alternate row k. 2 more. Thus, in the 26th row it will be k. 10, not 8.

31st row : * k. 1, p. 1, repeat from * 10 times, k. 1 in front and back of next st., k. 12, k. 1 in front and back of next st., p. 1, k. 1 to end of row.

32nd row : * p. 1, k. 1, repeat from * 10 times, k. 16, * k. 1, p. 1, repeat from * to end.

33rd row : * k. 1, p. 1, repeat from * 10 times, k. 1 in front and back of next st., k. 14, k. 1 in front and back of next st., * p. 1, k. 1, repeat to end.

Repeat the last 2 rows twice more, only having 2 more st. in the centre each time.

38th row : * k. 1, p. 1, repeat * 10 times, k. 22, * k. 1, p. 1, repeat from * to end.

39th row : * k. 1, p. 1, repeat * 10 times, k. 1 in front and back of the next st., k. 20, k. 1 in front and back of the next st., * k. 1, p. 1, repeat from * to end.

Repeat the last 2 rows twice more.

There will now be 28 st. in the centre.

44th row : k. 1, p. 1, repeat * 10 times, k. 28, * k. 1, p. 1, repeat to end.

Repeat the 44th row 7 times.

52nd row : * k. 1, p. 1, repeat * 10 times, k. 2 together, k. till 24 st. remain, k. 2 together, * k. 1, p. 1, repeat to end.

53rd row : * k. 1, p. 1, repeat * 10 times, k. till 22 remain, * k. 1., p. 1, repeat * to end.

Repeat the last 2 rows until 48 st. are left on the needle, k. 1, p. 1 on the 48 st. until 20 rows have been worked to correspond with the beginning. Cast off.

Sew the cast on to the cast-off stitches.

Make the other kneecap in the same way.

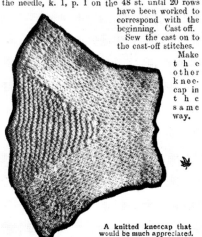

A knitted kneecap that would be much appreciated.

COMFORTS FOR OUR SOLDIERS AND SAILORS.
Woollen Helmets.

HAVE FOUR BONE NEEDLES, No. 9, pointed at each end. Cast on 90 stitches, 30 on each of three needles, very loosely. Work thus: Knit 3 stitches, purl 3. Go on in this manner round and round till you have done a piece 5 inches long. Then place on a piece of string 21 stitches; this should be 4 knit ribs and 3 purl ones. Put the remaining stitches on two needles (it is awkward at first to place them on one only; after a few inches you can get them on one), leaving off ribbing, and knit backwards and forwards quite plain for 38 rows; this will be about 4 inches. Now knit 15 stitches, take 2 together, knit remainder plain, next row the same; go on thus till you have reduced to about 42 stitches, then knit 9 stitches only, and take 2 together. Work thus until you have reduced to 25 stitches.

Now reduce four times in each row till 3 stitches remain. Now resume your four pins. Take up the loops at the ends of the plain rows, also the 21 stitches on the string; count them round; there should be 114 in all, including the 3 remaining on the pin; if there are too many or too few, take two together, or make one or two. Now rib round and round as you did at first, taking care that your ribs match on to those which were on the string. It is easiest to knit plain the first row till you arrive at those stitches, and then commence ribbing. Work thus for 2¼ inches. Cast off rather loosely.

This recipe was given in the *Queen* many years ago, but the Deep Sea Fishermen Mission issues a small book of useful comforts, including a similar helmet.

Right, top: How to knit a trench cap according to *Woman's Own* magazine, 13 January 1917.

Right, below: The Warleigh mitten with storm shield gauntlets featured in *The Queen* on 16 November 1918. They were useful mittens that could apparently be made by 'even the most inexperienced knitter'. The gauntlet covered the cuff of the tunic, thus effectively preventing cold and damp from penetrating up the arm.

Left: Pattern for a knitted helmet or balaclava, published in *The Queen* magazine on 15 August 1914 in the first fortnight of the war.

Trench Cap

MATERIAL required : 3½ ounces of 3-ply wheeling or Beehive double knitting wool, and No. 7 or 8 needles.

Cast on 100 stitches, 36 on one needle, and 32 on each of the others. Knit 1 row plain to set the stitches. Work in rounds of ribbing (knit 2, purl 2) for 4 inches.

Then knit 4 inches of plain knitting.

To finish the cap, decrease as follows :

On each needle : knit the 1st stitch, and knit the next 2 together. Knit up to the 3rd stitch from the end of the needle, slip this stitch, knit the next, and pass the slipped stitch over the knitted ; then knit the last stitch. Next knit 1 round of plain. Repeat these 2 rounds 6 times. Decrease on every round as above until there are only 23 stitches remaining. Break off the wool and thread it through the 23 stitches, and fasten off securely.

THE WARLEIGH MITTEN WITH STORM SHIELD GAUNTLETS.

THESE USEFUL MITTENS can be made in two sizes, and as they are simply worked in rows they can be easily made by even the most inexperienced knitter. The thumb and fingers are left free, and the gauntlet covers the cuff of the tunic, thus effectively preventing cold and damp from penetrating up the arm. Each of the pair can be used for either hand, an excellent expedient for equalising the wear. The materials required are two knitting needles, size 7, and two size 11 ; 2¾oz. Paton's Alloa Wheeling for the larger size— navy blue for sailors, khaki for soldiers. For the gauntlet : Use the larger needles and cast on 50 or 62 stitches according to size required. Always slip the first stitch and knit the last one in the row throughout the mitten. Work backwards and forwards always in a rib of 3 plain, 3 purl for 32 or 34 rows. It will be a help to mark the number of rows in tens on the right or outside of the work with a wool needle and white cotton, as both sides are the same. For the wrist : Use the smaller needles and reduce thus : Knit 3, purl 1, purl 2 together; repeat, leaving 42 or 52 stitches according to the number originally cast on. This is a front row. In the next row continue ribbing, but knit 2, purl 3, and in the return row knit 3, purl 2. Remember to continue slipping the first and knitting the last stitch. Repeat these 2 rows six or eight times. The ribs of 3 knitted stitches will be on the right or outer side of the mitten and will be a continuation of those in the gauntlet. For the palm : Alternately knit and purl 22 or 24 rows ; but in each purled row knit the first four and the last four stitches to make a flat margin for the thumb slit. For very long hands work 2 or 4 more of these rows. For the fist : Work in a rib of knit 2, purl 2 (in the return row purl 2, knit 2) for 6 or 8 rows, or more if required. Cast off, leaving an end of yarn to sew up this ribbing. Sew up the gauntlet and the wrist ribbing, work a row of double crochet round the thumb slit, putting two or three double stitches into the lower end. The smaller size is made with 1½oz. 4-ply fingering and needles 8 and 12. A variety in the gauntlet can be made in each size by ribbing it in knit 4, purl 2. In this case reduce thus : Knit 1, knit 2 together, knit 1, purl 2 ; repeat. The gauntlets can also be worked in the following pattern, which forms a very pretty rib : Brioche—Row 1. Make 1 by putting the row over the needle, slip 1, knit 2 together, repeat. Every row is the same. Work the required length with both sizes of the needles and continue as before directed.

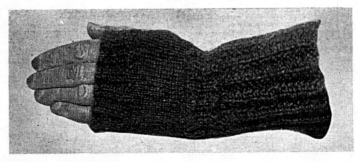

THE WARLEIGH MITTEN WITH STORM SHIELD GAUNTLETS.

KNITTED MITTEN WITH SHORT FIRST FINGER AND THUMB AND OPEN PALM (FOR RIFLE SHOOTING).

FOUR needles size 12; two extra needles for fingers; 2½oz. Alloa yarn. Cast 16 stitches on each of two needles and 20 on the third; total 52. For 24 rows knit 2, purl 2; then knit plainly 6 rows. Starting on first needle, increase for thumb by knitting 2, increase 1, knit 2, increase 1, finish the round plainly. Knit 2 rounds plain; knit 2, increase 1, knit 4 this time, increase 1; knit 4. Then cast off 9 stitches for open palm, knit to end of needles. Now, backwards and forwards, purl and plain alternately until there are 18 extra stitches for the thumb, made by increasing 2 stitches in every third row. In each third row knit 2 additional stitches between the stitches you increase; thus the second time of increasing there are 4, the third time 6,

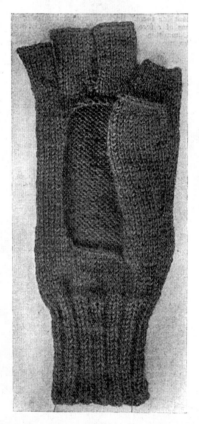

and so on. Take the 18 thumb stitches on to a piece of wool. There should now be 43 stitches left. Knit backwards and forwards alternately plain and purl 4 rows. Cast on 9 stitches to correspond with 9 cast off below. Knit 6 plain rounds.— First finger. Take 8 stitches off the front needle, 8 off the back one. Knit the 16 stitches plainly for 3 rows; cast off.— Second finger. Take 7 stitches off each of two needles and take up 4 in the gap by first finger. Knit 14 plain rows; cast off.—Third finger. Take 6 stitches off each of two needles, take up 4 in gap by second finger. Knit 15 plain rows; cast off.— Fourth finger. Take off the remaining 10 stitches, take up 4. Knit 10 plain rows; cast off. Take the 18 thumb stitches on to three needles; take up 2 stitches by first finger; cast off. A right and left hand mitten must be made, and the ends securely fastened off.

Left: Pattern for a knitted mitten with short first finger and thumb and open palm (for easy rifle shooting) from *The Queen,* 2 January 1915.

Right: A crochet balaclava cap which could be cleverly converted into a sleeping helmet, as featured in *The Queen* on 16 January 1915.

CROCHET BALACLAVA CAP AND SLEEPING HELMET COMBINED.

REQUIRED : 4oz. of Baldwin's four-ply fingering, khaki colour, and a medium fine bone crochet hook. Make 4 ch. into a ring, into which put 6 d. c.—2nd row. 2 d. c. into each of the 6 d. c., taking up both top portions of each stitch throughout.—3rd row. * 1 d. c. into next d. c., 2 d. c. into next d. c., * repeat.—4th row. * 1 d. c. into each of next 2 d. c., 2 d. c. into next d. c., * repeat.—5th row. 1 d. c. into each of next 3 d. c., 2 d. c. into next d. c., * repeat.— 6th row. * 1 d. c. into each of next 4 d. c., 2 d. c. into next d. c., * repeat.—7th row, 1 d. c. into each of next 5 d. c., 2 d. c. into next d. c., * repeat.—8th row. * 1 d. c. into each of next 6 d. c., 2 d. c. into next d. c., * repeat.—9th row. 1 d. c. into each d. c. up to the second of the 2 d. c., into which put 2 d. c., repeat this to the end of the row, and in every succeeding row increase the number of 1 d. c.s before the 2 d. c. by one until there are 117 stitches in the row. Then work 24 rows of the 117 stitches. In the next row 1 d. c. into each of the first 40, turn, * miss first d. c., 1 single into next, 1 d. c. into each of next 36 d. c., draw a loop through the last 2 d. c. of the 40, taking both together, and work off as 1 d. c., * turn and repeat for 10 rows.

Slip down the side of the 10 rows, and, turning out the other side of these 10 rows, work a row of 40 d. c. into the back of the 40 d. c., then turn and repeat the 10 rows on this side same as those on the front of this peak. Put the two edges together, and work a row of single stitch through both edges together thus : Insert the hook through the last stitch on the front and through the same stitch on the inside piece, draw a loop through both together and through the loop on the needle, draw this loop up closely, make 1 ch. softly, then insert the hook through next 2 corresponding stitches, and repeat the single stitch followed by 1 ch., and so on to the end of the peak. Continue round with 1 d. c. into each d. c. to the peak again, turn, * 2 d. c. into first and last d. c. 1 d. c. into each of the intervening d. c.s, turn, and repeat from * for 10 rows, then make sufficient chs. to bring the stitches up again to the 117, connect the two points, and continue working all round on the d. c.s and the chs. for the

117 d. c. Work on for a depth of 8 inches, and finish with a row of single stitch around the edge.

Make a little tuft for the centre of the crown by winding the wool 60 times around the tips of three fingers, tie through the centre tightly with a piece of the thread, then cut the ends of the loops evenly, and sew to the centre ring.

To fold the Cap.—Turn back the lower part in a line around the crown level with the beginning of the peak, then turn back again in a fold from the last row of increases around the crown. Pin the folds in place. Press with a hot iron over a piece of calico which has been slightly damped. This finishes a very comfortable cap, which by merely pulling down the folds over the neck and ears makes the best sleeping helmet known.

NOTE.—Unless this cap be made with the wool specified the size will not be correct, and for those who require them the following measurements should be adhered to : From the centre of the crown to the beginning of the peak, 9 inches; around the crown just above the peak, 24 inches ; width across opening under the peak, 8 inches ; depth of peak in centre, 2 inches ; from centre of the opening in front to the lower edge, 9 inches ; around the lower edge, 24 inches.

THE WORK-TABLE.

COMFORTS FOR OUR SOLDIERS AND SAILORS.

An Adjustable Abdominal Belt.

OUR SOLDIERS—and sailors, too—would find the belt in the sketch below particularly comfortable, as it is elastic, but not too "stretchy," whilst, being tied in front, is easily put on in any position and can be adjusted to any size. It thus obviates the objection so often urged against the belts knitted stocking-wise or wider at the lower than the upper part, the latter being not infrequently put on upside down, whilst the former are apt to stretch without any possibility of drawing them in or altering the size.

It was, however, mainly for the use of the Tommy suffering from abdominal wounds that the belt was designed. It can be put on when lying down either from front or back, and adjusted as required, and is so elastic that it will "give" with every movement. For this latter purpose it is better tied with very *soft* ribbon, but the soldier who is as yet unwounded may prefer a loop and buttons as fastenings. The former consists only of chain secured at the one end, whilst two or more buttons—and they should be quite flat ones—can be sewn on the other end so that the belt may be tightened if necessary. Safety-pins may also be mentioned in this connection, but the method is not one that would appeal to "Tommy Atkins"—and, if it did, the pins are not always to hand in the trenches.

The materials required for the belt are 3oz. khaki or grey soft fingering, 2 steel pins No. 10 or 12, according to whether you knit tightly or loosely, and 1½ yards of soft washing ribbon to tie with.

It is knitted lengthways, the experience of the maker being that belts are less "stretchy," and keep their shape better, than those knitted widthways. Begin with the strap part, for which cast on 4 stitches, and increase at the end of each row till you have 12 s itches on the pin, remembering to slip the first stitch in every row. You can make this strap wider if you like, the width being quite a matter of taste. The narrower one is less clumsy, but the wider one adds to the warmth. Increase at the *end* of every 2nd row, by knitting another stitch in the loop at the back of the stitch, in the last but one of the row, as there must always be a plain knitted stitch at the last stitch. Continue in this way till there are 72 stitches on the pins or the

belt is from 11 to 12 inches wide. Knit 5 plain rows without increasing in ordinary garter stitch, then knit 24, cast off 24, fairly loosely, and knit 24. Slip the first stitch always. In the next row again knit 24, cast-on 24—this is for the opening through which the end is passed—knit 24.

In the following row, when you are knitting the cast-on stitches, be very careful to pull the first and the last ones very close to the knitted ones they follow and precede, as otherwise you will have a sor of "ladder" at the ends of the opening. Knit the front portion of the belt in ribs, that is, work three rows in plain knitting, and purl the next three. This ribbing makes the belt more elastic and keeps it from stretching, as plain knitting is apt to do. Knit 60 such ribs, then knit 6 rows plain, and decrease to correspond with the other side, only this time you knit the two last stitches but one together, leaving one plain stitch after the decreasing to form the edge.

Decrease till you have 12 stitches on the pins, then knit the strap like the other and cast off.

Sew the ribbon on the ends very firmly, and baste the opening at each end if you find the stitches have not been drawn tightly enough together.

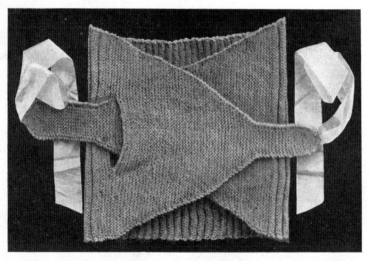

AN ADJUSTABLE ABDOMINAL BELT.

Convolvulus.

Part 1, for the first of the pair, in which the spiral lines rise to the right as the work grows.

Rounds one to five.—Knit 4, purl 1; repeat. Rounds six to ten.—Knit 3, *, purl 1, knit 4: repeat from *, at the end purl 1, knit 1. Rounds eleven to fifteen.—Knit 2, *, purl 1.

Left: An adjustable abdominal belt used mainly for support and protection by men suffering from abdominal wounds, as featured in *The Queen* on 13 February 1915.

Right: Warleigh leggings and sleeves were ideal comforts, as the leggings could be worn under puttees or over ordinary stockings, while the sleeves served a triple purpose – they could be turned back over wrists, drawn over the hands or clasped in fists. The pattern, which was published in *The Queen* on 17 April 1915, included a brightly coloured band on one end to signify which was the top edge.

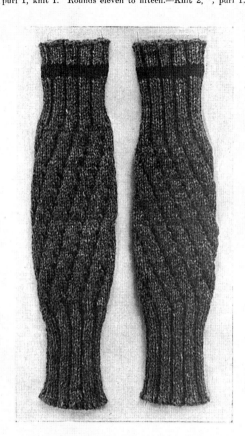

knit 4; repeat from *, at the end purl 1, knit 2. Rounds sixteen to twenty.—Knit 1, *, purl 1, knit 4; repeat from *, at the end purl 1, knit 3. Rounds twenty-one to twenty-five.— Purl 1, knit 4; repeat. Repeat from round one.

Part 2, for the second of the pair, in which the spiral lines rise to the left as the work grows.

Rounds one to five.—Purl 1, knit 4; repeat. Rounds six to ten.—Knit 1, *, purl 1, knit 4; repeat from *, at the end purl 1, knit 3. Rounds eleven to fifteen.—Knit 2, *, purl 1, knit 4; repeat from *, at the end purl 1, knit 2. Rounds sixteen to twenty.—Knit 3, *, purl 1, knit 4; repeat from *, at the end purl 1, knit 1. Rounds twenty-one to twenty-five.—Knit 4, purl 1; repeat. Then repeat from round one.

When the spiral part is finished rib thirty rounds as at the top, omitting the coloured band and cast off loosely.

To make these leggings or sleeves larger or smaller, cast on 10 or 5 stitches more or fewer. They can be made for women and children in 4 ply fingering, with needles size 9.

HENRIETTA WARLEIGH.

MITTENS FOR THE TROOPS.

The D.G.V.O., as Sir Edward Ward is already known, in virtue of his appointment as Director General of Voluntary Organisations, has asked for mittens and mufflers for the troops. The former are of given dimensions, and as these vary from those usually employed, it may help readers to give directions for their making.

The main provision is that the length should be 8 inches, this reaching from the first knuckle to the end of the wrist part, which should be ribbed; the rest of the mitten is plain, with a ribbed border at the top and thumb. The width when finished at the top should be 7 inches.

A fairly coarse wool, 3-ply alloa yarn or fingering should be chosen, with four No. 12 needles. The colour should be the "drab," which in service parlance represents the familiar khaki shades. As the thickness of the wool chosen (and it is not a vital matter, though naturally too fine a one reduces the desired warmth) affects the directions, it seems better to gives these more by measurement than by the usual method of the number of rows; for the measurements of the result is the all-important matter in regulation things, and this as any one who knits knows, does depend in greater or less degree on the wool chosen, which is my excuse for the somewhat unconventional manner in which the following directions are given:

To commence, cast on 16 stitches on each three needles, o· 20 on one, if the wool is on the fine side, making a total of 48 in the usual quality, or 52 in the fine. Knit 2 plain, 2 purl round and round until the cuff measures 3 inches long. Then knit all plain for another inch, when the time has come to start the thumb. This is worked entirely in one with the hand, not an added affair as in the more usual affair, and the first needle (distinguished by the fact that the end of the cuff from which it started still has the unfinished end of wool hanging from it), bears the whole responsibility for it. In starting this row, then, knit 2, make a stitch by knitting through the wool at the base,

THE REGULATION MITTEN

knit 2, make another stitch, and continue plainly around the rest of the needles. Knit two rows plain. Then on the first needle knit 2 again; make a stitch; knit 4; make a stitch, and continue once more to the end of the row. Again knit two plain rows. Then on the first needle knit 2; make one, knit 6, make one, and continue as before. Go on with this plan, making two stitches in every third row with a space increasing by two stitches in between, until this number has reached 18. Then knit the two following rows, and take off these 18 stitches on to a separate piece of wool, tying it up to keep safely until needed.

Then knit plainly around (excluding these 18 stitches) until an additional half inch is gained in length, then 1 inch 2 plain 2 purl for the ribbed border, and cast off very loosely.

Take the 18 stitches up on three needles, 6 on each. Make two extra stitches at the beginning of the first needle (which will give it 8), and knit half an inch plain and 1 inch rib; cast off loosely, and you have the complete mitten.

The casting off looks better if done from the back instead of the front, the obvious "plait" effect being thus avoided; and this has been done in the example illustrated, but it is really a matter of little moment.

With ordinary wool 2oz. suffices for a pair of mittens, so they are both quickly and cheaply made.

Left: The regulation mitten, which was made according to directions given by Sir Edward Ward, Director General of Voluntary Organisations. Published in *The Queen,* 23 October 1915.

Right, top: The pattern for a knitted cardigan for soldiers was featured in *The Queen,* 30 October 1915.

Right: Published in *The Queen* on 12 February 1916, this pattern is for a knitted rifle glove, leaving the thumb and forefinger free.

DIRECTIONS FOR KNITTING A CARDIGAN JACKET IN PLAIN KNITTING.

Materials Required.—Two bone needles No. 9, 2 steel needles No. 15 for the border, 14oz. of 4-ply fingering wool.

For the back.—Cast 80 stitches on the bone needles and knit plain until you can count 100 ribs (200 rows). Then knit 2 together at the beginning and end of each row until the stitches are reduced to 40; cast off.

For the fronts.—Cast on 50 stitches, knit plain until you can count 70 ribs (140 rows); next row knit 47, knit 2 together, knit 1; next row knit 1, knit 2 together, knit 46; repeat these rows until the stitches are reduced to 40; this is for the armhole. Knit plain on the 40 stitches until you can count 85 ribs from the beginning, then on the opposite side from the armhole begin to slope away for the neck. To do this knit 1, knit 2 together at the beginning of the row only, that is to say in every alternate row; continue to do this until the front is finished. When you can count 95 ribs from the beginning you must increase again at the armhole side. To do this make 1, knit 1 at the end of the row, and knit 1, make 1 at the beginning of the next row; do this for 10 rows. You will now be able to count 100 ribs from the beginning. Now knit 2 together every row on the armhole side while you continue to knit 2 together every alternate row at the neck side until all the stitches are worked off. Sew the fronts to the back at the shoulders and under the arms.

For the sleeves.—Cast on 48 stitches, knit 2 plain, 2 purl for 20 rows; then knit plain for 5 ribs (10 rows); next row increase 1 stitch at each end, and do this every 5th rib (10th row) until you have 80 stitches on the needle. When you can count 85 ribs from the end of the cuff, decrease 1 stitch at the beginning and end of each row until the stitches are reduced to 40; cast off.

Make a border in finer knitting to go all round the fronts and neck and take the buttons and buttonholes. To do this cast 18 stitches on the steel needles and knit plain. When you have done a certain length it is best to sew it on the coat as you go along, beginning with the button side. Then you will be able to see when to begin the buttonholes. For these knit 12, cast off 3, knit 3, and the next row knit 3, cast on 3, knit 12. Knit 20 ribs (40 rows) between each buttonhole. There should be 6 buttonholes down the front.   MAUD E. HANSELL.

A CARDIGAN JACKET IN PLAIN KNITTING.

KNITTED RIFLE GLOVE.

ONE ounce of 4-ply fingering will be sufficient for this very useful article, as only the right hand glove is required, the left being made in the usual way. Six knitting needles No. 12 are used in making.

KNITTED RIFLE GLOVE.

Cast 14 stitches on each of two needles and 16 on the third. Join round and knit first row plain. In second row knit 1, purl 1 alternately to start the ribbing, of which you make 27 rows. 28th row. Knit plain.—29th row. Knit plain.—30th row. Knit 1, purl 1 alternately.—31st row. Knit 8, knit 1 into each side of next stitch (this increases by one at the back of the thumb, which we are now starting), knit 1, knit twice into next stitch (this increases by one at the front of the thumb), knit remainder of row.—32nd row. *There are no increases in this row nor in the alternate rows following. Knit 1, purl 1. In this row the stitches that were purled in the 30th row must be purled in the increasing stitches. Knit the second to preserve the pattern, which consists of alternate stripes of plain knitting and sand stitch. 33rd row. Knit plain, increasing in the first increasing stitch at the back of the thumb and in the last increasing stitch at the front*. Repeat these two rows until in the 42nd row there are 23 stitches on the thumb part. Work five rows without increase. Take the other two needles, and, taking off all but the thumb stitches on these, arrange the 23 stitches on three needles, 8 on the first and second, and 7 on the third. Cast on 3, and joining round, work a row in pattern working into the 3 cast on. Take over the cast on stitches on the 4th needle and continue around to the beginning of next row. Knit 2 together, knit 2 together, then work remainder of row in pattern. Decrease in next row in the same way, then work 10 rows of the 22 stitches in pattern. Next five rows in ribbing, 1 p, 1 k; cast off. Take over the 8 stitches before the thumb (that is at the back of it), fasten the thread and raise the 3 cast on at the base of the thumb, knit in pattern next 5 on same needle—16 on this needle in all. This will be the needle on which the forefinger will be formed. Divide remainder on two needles and work around in pattern for 20 rounds. Now take the spare needles and divide the 16 on the first needle among two others—6 on each of two, 4 on the third, cast on 4, and forming into a round work 11 rounds in pattern and 4 rounds of ribbing as in the thumb, then cast off.

Divide the remaining stitches equally on three needles, raising the 4 at the base of the forefinger and continue working for thirty rounds. Decrease for the top by knitting 2 together in the plain row after every 3rd stitch. In next round take the 2 knit stitches together. In next decrease after every 2nd stitch, then knit every 2 together until the stitches are reduced to 4. Cast off and draw the end of the thread through the last stitch. Turn the glove inside out and sew up the top closely with the end of thread.

This glove must not be knitted with too thick woollen thread, for if at all clumsy it would impede the free motion of the hand when engaged in firing the rifle.

CROCHET OPERATION BED JACKET.

REQUIRED, 1½lb. of 4-ply soft fingering, a medium fine bone crochet hook, five half-inch pearl buttons, about 3 yards of wide tape, and the paper pattern supplied by the *Queen* Paper Pattern Department, Windsor House, Bream's Buildings, E.C.

Commencing at the centre back, make 148ch, turn.—1st row. 1tr into the 145th ch (this stands for the 2nd tr, the 3ch left at the beginning represents the first tr), 1tr into each ch to the end for 146tr in the row.—2nd row. 1dc into the first tr, taking up each top portions of each stitch throughout, 2ch (this dc and 2ch represent the first tr in each row), 1tr into each tr.—3rd row. 1dc into first tr, 2ch, 1tr into each tr, 1 single into next tr, turn.—22nd and 23rd 7th row. 1dc into the first tr, 1tr into each tr except the last tr, into which put 2tr, 13ch.—8th row. 1tr into the 16th ch, 1tr into each of the following 15ch and into each tr to the end. There are now 164tr in the row, counting the

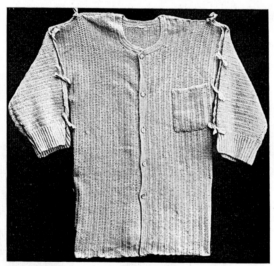

CROCHET OPERATION BED JACKET.

first 3ch as a tr.—9th row. 1dc into first tr, 2ch, 1tr into each tr to the top.—10th row. Miss the first tr, 1dc into the second tr, 2ch, 1tr into each tr to the end.—11th, 13th, 15th, 17th, and 21st rows. 1dc into first tr, 2ch, 1tr into each tr to the end.—12th, 14th, 16th, 18th, and 20th rows. Same as the 10th. There are now 158tr.—22nd and 23rd rows. Work without decreasing.—24th row. 1dc into first tr, 2ch, 1tr into each of next 15tr, 1 short tr into next tr, 1dc into next tr, 1 single into next tr, turn.—25th row. Slip-stitch up to the first tr, into which put a dc, 1tr into each tr to the top; fasten and cut off the thread. Continuation of the 24th and 25th rows.—24th. Fasten the thread to the 37th tr from the top of the 23rd row with a dc, 1 short tr into next tr, 1tr into each tr to the end.—25th. 1dc into first tr, 2ch, 1tr into each tr until within 3tr from the end; into the first of these put 1 short tr. 1dc into the next, 1 single into next; fasten the thread and cut it.—26th row. Fasten the thread to the first stitch at top of 25th row with a tr, and put a tr into each of the following 55tr; turn. This is the first sleeve row.—27th row. * Miss first tr, 1dc into second tr, 2ch, 1tr into each tr to the end.—23rd row. 1dc into first tr, 2ch, 1tr into each tr.* Repeat these 2 rows three times more, when the stitches will be reduced to 50. Then work 18 rows without decrease. In the following rows decrease as before on the same side, that is the lower or under side of sleeve. There are 34 rows in the sleeve.

The ribbed cuff.—1dc into last tr, 17ch, turn; 1dc into 16th ch and 1dc into each ch, that is 15dc, 1dc into each of next 2tr, turn; * 1dc into each dc, turn (take up only the back portion of each dc); 1ch, 1dc into each dc, taking up the back portion of each stitch; 1dc into each of next 2tr, taking both top portions; * repeat until all the trs have been worked. Fasten the thread and cut it. This completes one-half of the back. Fasten the thread again to the other side of the foundation ch and work the 146tr into it, then form the other half to correspond.

The front.—137ch, turn.—1st row. 1tr into the 134th ch and 1tr into each ch for 135tr.—2nd row. Working the first tr always as in the back portion, put 1tr into each tr.—3rd row. * 2tr into first tr, 1tr into each remaining tr.—4th row. 1tr into each tr; * repeat once.—7th row. Fasten the thread and cut it, then make 25ch, and with the loop on the needle fasten the thread again to the end of the 6th row, with 2tr into the first tr and 1tr into each tr to the end.—8th row. 1tr into each tr and into each of the 25ch. There are now 164tr in the row.—9th row. * Miss first tr, 1tr into each tr.—10th row. 1tr into each tr; * repeat these 2 rows six times more.—23rd, 24th, and 25th rows. 1tr into each tr (without decrease).—25th row. Fasten the thread to the 54th tr from the top of the 25th row with a tr, and work the sleeve exactly as in the back portion, taking care to make the decreases at the lower edge. The shoulder line must be kept straight. Work the other front to correspond. Now join the three parts together in the under-arm and side seam. Put the two edges together, making a row of single stitch through corresponding stitches on the wrong side. Overlap the front half of the sleeve on the back portion in a seam of 2 inches; pin these in place. Then, commencing at the lower edge of the right front, work a row of dc up the front edge, around the neck, and down the left front edge; turn, and work a second row into the first, then a third row, decreasing around the neck by taking every 3rd and 4th dc together, and working these two off as 1dc. At the top of the left front form the first button-hole by making 3ch after the 2nd dc, * miss next 3 dc, then 23dc into next 20dc; form another buttonhole by 3ch, and repeat from * until five buttonholes are formed, then finish the row with dc. Work 2 rows more of dc, putting 1dc into each ch over the buttonholes, 2dc into each corner stitch, and decreasing as before around the neck. Cut the

tape into even lengths and sew in place on the sleeves; sew on the buttons.

The pocket is not absolutely necessary, but is a great convenience, and where possible should be added. It is composed of 12 rows of 27trs, and finished at the top with 2 rows of dc, then sewn in place, using the woollen thread for the purpose.

In washing woollen crochet or knitted garments warm water should always be used, with plenty of pure white soap dissolved in it, and if a teaspoonful of glycerine be added to each quart of the rinsing water it improves the softness and prevents shrinking.

The paper pattern will be found a great help to the inexperienced worker, as she can place her work over it from time to time to see if she is keeping within the measurements. It also enables her to make one of these much-needed articles from any make of thread, as by making a length of chain stitches equal to the length and of the centre back or front, and then following, in a general way, the foregoing directions, a well-fitting garment is assured.

Garments for convalescents were as common as those for active troops. This pattern for a crocheted bed jacket for wounded men was published in *The Queen*, 13 November 1915.

WARM CROCHET UNDER-WAISTCOAT FOR OFFICERS.

FOR USE IN COLD COUNTRIES these waistcoats worn under the tunic give great warmth without weight. They are furnished with two deep pockets which will be found handy for containing documents, letters, &c.

Three-quarters of a pound of double knitting, 6-ply, or double Berlin wool (English made) with a fine bone crochet hook will be required, also half a dozen buttons and some button-hole twist. The waistcoat illustrated here was made with natural colour double knitting wool.

Commence by making a chain of 164 stitches.—1st row. Draw a loop through the second stitch from the needle, thread over the hook and draw through the two loops on the needle, 1 ch, draw a loop through the back of the 1 ch, another through the side of the dc, retaining all on the needle, draw a loop through each of next 2 ch. There are now five loops on the needle, thread over the hook and draw through the five loops together, make 1 ch, * draw a loop through the back of the 1 ch, another through the side loop of last stitch (called " a marguerite "), one through each of next 2 ch ; there are five loops on the needle, thread over the hook and draw through all five loops together, 1 ch *. Repeat to the end.—2nd row. Along the edge of last row there are two chain stitches in each marguerite, make 1 ch at the turning, then put 1 dc into each of the chain stitches on edge of last row.

Repeat these two rows alternately until there are five rows of the marguerites. In the next row, the dc row, a buttonhole is formed, thus, 1 ch at the turning, 1 dc into each of next 2 ch on edge of next marguerite, 3 ch, pass over next 3 ch, 1 dc into each of following stitches to the end. In next row of marguerites continue taking up each of the 3 ch over the buttonhole as in the remainder of the row.

Form a similar buttonhole after every third row of marguerites until there are six buttonholes in all. Work until the fourteenth row of dc is finished. Cut the thread and make two pocket pieces thus, 27 ch, turn and make 26 dc into these chs, work two rows more of the 26 dc, then 7 rows of 26 trs, and finally three rows of dc. Make another like this. Fasten the thread to the beginning of next row of marguerites and form 12 of them as before. Take up the pocket piece and place it in position behind, pass over first two dc on the pocket piece and continue working the marguerites into the dc on edge of the pocket piece until nine marguerites are worked on it. Pass over the corresponding number of dc on the front of the waist-coat and work next marguerites into the dc on the front and around to the other side of the waistcoat, where you place the other pocket piece in position and work in a similar manner, taking care to have the pocket 12 marguerites from the front edge.

Work next dc row, then the following row of marguerites as far as the 25th marguerite, * turn without the dc, miss 1 ch, 1 dc into each ch. Turn, 1 marguerite into each 2 ch for 23 in the row, * repeat, decreasing by 2 marguerites in each of next three rows of marguerites. * In the next row

of dc take up last two stitches together. (This starts the decreasing for the neck.) Miss this stitch when making the following row of marguerites, of which there should be 15 in the row, * repeat twice more. Work next row of marguerites without decrease (13). In the four following rows of marguerites, decrease one on the front edge, and increase one at the armhole side in each row, having 12 marguerites in each of these rows. End with the row of dc. Work the other front to correspond, continuing with the buttonholes until the sixth is formed.

For the back, miss 2 dc. Fasten the thread and work the marguerites across to the 3rd dc from the other front, turn, miss first stitch, 1 dc into each ch to opposite end, taking last 2 together. On this row work the marguerites for the back until there are 12 rows of the marguerites. Work six more rows decreasing by one at each side and ending with the row of dc.

Place the shoulder seams together with the wrong side turned out. Join together with a row of single stitch worked closely. Join the other shoulder seams. Now work a row of dc up the right front edge, around the neck and down the other front edge. Fasten the thread and cut it. Into the row of dc work a row of single stitch, commencing at the first dc, thus—draw a loop through the dc, pull this loop through the loop on the needle, tightly, make 1 ch loosely, * draw a loop through next dc and pull this loop through that on the hook, tightly, make 1 loose ch *. Repeat into every dc. Work

WARM CROCHET UNDER-WAISTCOAT FOR OFFICERS.

these two rows around each armhole and th row of single stitch on edge of each pocket.

With buttonhole twist of the same colour as the woollen thread work each buttonhole. Sew on the buttons to correspond. Then with a piece of the woollen thread top-sew the pocket piece on the back of each front, keeping it perfectly flat and smooth. This completes a warm, useful waistcoat.

Pattern published in *The Queen*, 5 June 1916, for a warm crochet under-waistcoat for officers, to be worn under the tunic to give warmth without weight. There are also two deep pockets, handy for containing items such as documents and letters.

THE WORK-TABLE.

NEW WORK BY MRS ELLIOTT.

Scarves.

THESE ARE QUICKLY WORKED on the prepared boards made especially for the purpose. By using a folding board the work does not take up so much room, and is altogether more handy. On these boards a scarf can be made in five different widths from 4 to 10 inches. The work is much quicker than either crochet or knitting. On the same boards the double scarves so much used for cold weather can be made. They take more wool, but are as quickly worked. The boards are registered, and supplied by Pearsall's firm, of Little Britain.

The materials required are a folding board, a bodkin, a kindergarten needle, a wool needle with a blunt point, and a sharp pair of scissors. Baldwin's silk motor wools, Lady Betty Berry, and merino wools make lovely soft and fine scarves. Any other quality can, of course, be used; 3oz. of wool will make a long scarf worked from side to side on the case. Where a double scarf is made it will require a little more.

Scarf No. 1.

Worked with merino wool and stripes of colour at the ends, 3¾oz yards of each colour are required; those used were dark maroon, light blue, black, maize, sage green. Also of dark plain colour and cardinal, about 30 yards.

Take the warp threads with the white wool, first count the number of notches at the end of the board, the one under the first and the last notches, and all between the notches.

Measure the full length of the board, add 3½ inches, double the length, and cut it off. Remember to cut all lengths by the first one cut, never from any other; this must always be measured, or you will have no two the same length.

Place the board full length flat on the table, the ends of the wool to the right and left. Take one length of wool, put the two ends together, slip the ends on the left hand under the far edge of the board, and place the double end over to catch close to the wire. Pass the upper wool along the case, also the under one to the right-hand notch, and tie them under all worked over. When a depth of 3 inches is worked take the coloured stripes, work first 5 rows of dark maroon, then 5 of maize, 5 of sage green, 3 of brown, 5 green, 5 maize, 3 of maroon, 5 claret; 1½ inches in cardinal, 5 rows of claret, 3 of maroon, 3 of maize, 5 green, 6 brown, 5 green, 3 maize, 2 maroon, 2 blue, 3 maroon, 3 black, a stripe ½ inch wide of claret, ½ inch brown, 3 maroon, 3 maize, and 5 maroon. Work with white to the fold in the board.

Open the board, push the needles up until they meet those on the other side. Work over these and then to the extreme end of the board over the edge and on the other side; press the two first rows close to the edge. Remove the first needle, loosen the fasteners in rotation, pull out the needle carefully, take the washers, and replace the needle in the fasteners, hold the two ends of the fastener close, and pass it through the washer and in the eyelet on the reverse side of the board. Press each fastener open as it is replaced. Measure where the coloured stripes are to come on this board, work with white to that point. Then repeat the coloured stripes and finish with white to the end; there fasten off. Draw the needles out, then untie the warp threads. Lay the scarf full length flat on the table, with the bodkin run two lengths of the wool through the loops that were withdrawn from the needle, and regulate the loops where required.

FOR THE FRINGE.—Wind the white wool forty times round the width of the board, cut it on each edge. Take two lengths, put the ends together, and loop these over the first two rows worked, and the warp threads at the end. Work two lengths into every two loops across the board. The threads that were run through the loops on the needles should be passed through the knot on every fringe next to it. Then trim the edges of the fringe.

A Double Scarf.

For a double scarf 60 inches in length, the warp threads must be cut double the length it is required; these are put over the notches at one end in the manner described in No. 1 exactly in the centre of the full length of each board. They must be carried down to the opposite notch, there tied with one to together. When all are placed and tied over the notch the extra length of thread is rolled very carefully together in a piece of soft muslin, then is tied down to the end of the board. Cover this end carefully while working.

Fasten the threads in their places by four cross threads, as described above, and work at the end with no ties. When the work requires moving, untie the ends gently, press it down

SCARF No. 1.

under in the corresponding notch. Lay a length in the same manner over the near wire and just under it. See these serve as firm and even, but not tight. Lay a strand of wool in the same way on the notch close to the two end wires, then a alternate notches between them. Tie all the ends at the right end in corresponding notches, see all straight and even. Then take a length of wool and tie it across the board where it is folded, tie it on the near side in a bow. Tie another length in the same manner at each end, halfway between this to and the end.

METHOD OF WORKING.—Fold the board, place it on the table the bodkin with it.—1st row. Commence on the right-hand side close to the five on the notches, pass the needle under the wire and its threads, *over the next thread, under the following and repeat from* *twice; then draw the wool and needle on three-quarters of a yard, take up the remainder of the stitches in the same way. The last stitch will be an over one; draw out the full length, leaving 3 inches at the end. Take up the three ends with the hands and pull this row straight and tight. See the thread is close to the notches.—2nd row. Commence with an under stitch, work over every row worked under, and under all worked over. When a few stitches have been worked gently draw the wool out its full length until it is tight on the edge; then take up the remainder and finish the row. These two rows are the only difficult ones.—3rd and following rows. Work over all stitches worked under, and from the board, leaving a good inch of work in its place on the board. Take the threads, lay again in the same place at the top, and tie again. Cover the work and with a handkerchief and work the remainder. The needles are not used for the sides. When working round the boards place a thread of the wool over each side, as already described, then make a tiny cut between the last notch and the outside edge of the board. Do this on each side, place a warp thread on each of these little cuts.

It has a very good effect to have a side stripe in a contrasting colour. For instance, a white scarf with a coloured stripe of mauve up each side is good. Lay 6 threads in white on each side, then 10 in colour on each side, and the *intermediate* notches in white. The woof can be worked with single or double wool if a three ply. I recommend double wool. Work in serge stitch, and keep the 2 threads untwisted and together, but not over each other. Commence close to the edge where the loops are on the notches.—1st row. Take up the 2 first threads on the needle, then over 2, under 2 alternately, draw the wool out halfway, leaving an end of 3 inches in length. When the side is covered turn the board over and work the other side to the last stitch, where there will be the extra thread left.

When all the wool is arranged, take the needle under it. Turn the board. Take up the next one of the 2 first stitches over the 2 next. The needle of your under stitches must now come up in the centre of the under stitches of last row, and the needle of your over stitches go down in the centre of every over stitch of last row. Follow this row throughout and you will have your serge stitch. It may be necessary to work a row on each side to replace the space made by removing the board, but with the extra warp threads on the margin of the board this should not be necessary. Remove the work as directed in Scarf No. 1, and add a fringe at each end.

There are good patterns and directions given for scarves in my handbooks of Pearsall's "Home Weaving."

Instructions for a crocheted sock and knitted spencer for a nurse, as recommended by *The Queen* magazine in early September 1914. The magazine stresses that 'while attending to the wants of soldiers at the front we must not forget the no less brave women who attend them, and who may not have the opportunity of supplying themselves with all the comforts necessary for their welfare while attending to their duties through the coming winter during their trying ordeal'.

THE WORK-TABLE.

SOLDIERS' AND NURSES' COMFORTS—CROCHETED SOCKS.

CROCHETED SOCKS for our soldiers at the front are much quicker and easier to make than knitted ones; they are also more durable, as there can be no "running" of the stitches if one stitch happens to get broken, and are very easy to repair on this account. An expert worker can easily make a couple of pairs in a day. Four ounces of white or natural colour four-ply fingering and a No. 1 steel crochet hook are required. For the ribbing make 26 ch. Turn, miss 1 ch., and form 25 d. c. into the remaining chs. Turn, 1 ch., 1 d. c. into each d. c., taking up that portion of each top stitch next to the first finger of the left hand. * Repeat for 56 rows, or 28 ribs. Place the first and last rows together and join with a row of d. c. through corresponding stitches. Turn this top right side out, and continue with taking up the stitch along one side at the end of each row, and work d. c. into it in this way : * draw a loop through the stitch, thread over the needle and through the loop, thread over the needle and through the two loops now on the needle. *Repeat. There should be 56 d. c. in the round. Work 38 rows of this stitch, taking up both portions of the top stitch throughout. In the 39th row work as far as the 28th d. c., * turn with 1 ch., and repeat the stitch into each of these 28 * Repeat for 12 rows in all. Fold this heel piece in two and join the two halves of last row with a row of single stitch through corresponding stitches, thus : * insert the hook through the top of last stitch and through the first, draw a loop through these and the loop on the needle, make 1 ch., * repeat through the second and twenty-seventh d. c., and so on to the end. Fasten the thread recurely, and work the end in and out through a few stitches. Now fasten the thread to the first stitch on the heel, and, taking up every stitch around, work the d. c. into it; continue working into the 28th d. c. at the beginning of the heel. In the next row decrease one at each side of the 28 on the front by taking up two stitches together. Decrease in this way every second round three times more, when the stitches should be reduced to 44. Work 32 rounds in all from the side of the heel. Fold this foot in two with the centre of the heel in a line with the centre of the sole. Decrease in next round by taking the 22nd and 23rd stitches together and the 43rd and 44th. Work next round without decrease, then decrease in next and alter-

nate rows three times more. Turn the sock inside out, and join the top part as you did the heel. If the sock be washed in tepid water, dried, and pressed before wearing, it will last much longer, and be soft and extremely comfortable.

A Knitted Spencer for Nurses.

While attending to the wants of the soldiers at the front we must not forget the no less brave women who attend them, and who may not have the opportunity of supplying themselves with all the comforts necessary for their welfare while attending to their duties through the coming winter during their trying ordeal. The knitted spencer is a garment of which there should be a very liberal supply in the outfit of every nurse. Being so very light they take up but little space, and while affording a grateful warmth, they protect the wearer from the sudden chills to which she will certainly be exposed. Three ounces of white Shetland wool, a set of coarse steel needles, and a set of fine needles will be required, with a yard and a quarter of inch-wide white washing silk riband for casing the fronts, and a similar length of narrow riband for the waist draw-string.

Commence at the lower edge. With the coarse set of needles cast 48 stitches on the first, 28 on the second, 48 on the third. Knit ten rows plainly on these stitches, working rather loosely but even. Every alternate row being purled, every alternate row being purled. 11th row. * Knit 2 together, thread over, * repeat, knitting last two together. 12th row. Knit 1, * knit 32, 1 over, knit 1, * repeat.—13th and 14th rows. Knit plain.—15th row. Knit 16, 1 over, knit 32, 1 over, knit 28, 1 over, knit 32, 1 over, knit 16.—16th row. Knit plain, knitting each over. Every alternate row following is knit plain, like the 16th. 17th row. Knit 17, 1 over, knit 32, 1 over, knit 29 1 over, knit 32, 1 over, knit 30. —19th row. Knit 18, 1 over, knit 32, 1 over, knit 30, 1 over, knit 32, 1 over, knit 32.—21st row. Knit 19, 1 over, knit 32, 1 over, knit 31, 1 over, knit 32, 1 over, knit 19.—23rd row. Knit 20, 1 over, knit 32, 1 over, knit 32, 1 over, knit 32, 1 over, knit 20.—25th row. Knit 21, 1 over, knit 32, 1 over, knit 33, 1 over, knit 32, 1 over, knit 21.—27th row. Knit 22, 1 over, knit 32, 1 over, knit 34, 1 over, knit 32, 1 over, knit 22.—29th row. Knit 23, 1 over, knit 32, 1 over, knit 35, 1 over, knit 32, 1 over, knit 23.—31st row. Knit 24, 1 over, knit 32, 1 over, knit 36, 1 over, knit 32, 1 over, knit 24.—33rd row. Knit 25, 1 over, knit 32, 1 over, knit 37, 1 over, knit 32, 1 over, knit 25. —35th row. Knit 26, 1 over, knit 32, 1 over, knit 38, 1 over, knit 32, 1 over, knit 26.—37th row. Knit 27, 1 over, knit 32, 1 over, knit 39, 1 over, knit 32, 1 over, knit 27.—39th row.

Knit 28, 1 over, knit 32, 1 over, knit 40, 1 over, knit 32, 1 over, knit 28.—41st row. Knit 29, 1 over, knit 32, 1 over, knit 41, 1 over, knit 32, 1 over, knit 29.— 43rd row. Knit 30, 1 over, knit 32, 1 over, knit 42, 1 over, knit 32, 1 over, knit 30.—45th row. Knit 31, 1 over, knit 32, 1 over, knit 43, 1 over, knit 32, 1 over, knit 31.—46th row. Knit 31, then the over and next 12, put the remaining stitches over on the second needle, and leave these for the present.

On the 44 stitches on the first needle work 32 rows plain. 79th row. Knit the first 15 stitches with a fine needle and leave them for the present. Work six more rows on the remaining 29 with the coarse needles, then cast these off. Knit the next 29 and the following over on a spare needle, and leave them for the present. These 21 stitches are afterwards taken into the sleeve. Knit next 43. and form 24 rows on them, then 16 rows more, decreasing one at the beginning of every row by knitting two together. This reduces the stitches to 27. Knit these 27 on a fine needle and leave them.

Knit the other front exactly like the first, and leave the stitches for the sleeve as at the other side.

You have now three sections for the neck on the fine needles. Work 1 plain 1 purl alternately on first needle, pick up the stitches at the end of the additional six rows on this front, work the second needle and pick up next six rows on the second front, then the third needle is continuous row. Form six rows of ribbing and cast off. Sew up the shoulder seams, using the same kind of thread.

Pick up the stitches around the arm-hole, using two of the coarse needles ; divide them evenly. Take over 11 of the 21 left on the needle for the sleeve, so that the joining for the sleeve may come in the centre of these stitches. Knit 40 rows backwards and forwards, then 40 more in which you decrease one at each side in every third row. Finish the sleeve with the ribbing as for the neck. Sew up the seam. Case both front edges with the riband and sew on a few waist fasteners. Insert the narrow riband through the beading at the waist to complete this useful garment.

A VALUABLE BATCH OF DIRECTIONS FOR KNITTING COMFORTS FOR MEN ON LAND AND ON SEA.

IT does not seem really possible to have too many different styles of socks and headgear to suit the fastidious fancies of the friends of those going to the front and are not yet accustomed to rough it. The choice contained in the three following leaflets is very attractive. Both the cosiness of the models illustrated and their becoming fit have been studied as closely as possible in such

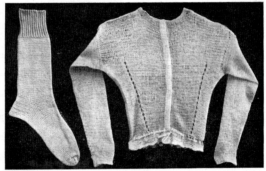

A CROCHETED SOCK AND NURSE'S SPENCER.

matters. As an instance, see the helmet with cap pieces described in Beehive Knitting Leaflet No. 17. It has a ribbed band round the face opening and the neck, whilst across the top of the head between two side pieces runs a panel shaped to the head like the heel of a stocking ; the two drooping flaps for chest and back hang comfortably independently from each other, thus leaving the arms and shoulders perfectly free. The second example on the contrary is in plain knitting all in one straight piece, and looks on the diagram like a large heel-less stocking, with an opening for the face towards the pointed piece standing for the top. This easy type is quickly slipped over the head, and is arranged round the neck as a full round collarette ready for stormy weather.

Next come longer directions for knitting a Cardigan or coat sweater provided with capacious pockets. A seaman's jersey to be knitted with 3 ply wheeling in a reliable shade of navy blue which stands water, recommends itself equally well to yacht and sportsmen.

Knitters who do not care to undertake either long or heavy work will in preference turn their attention to the varied recipes for fringed neck scarves in plain ribbed knitting, body belts, socks either ribbed, heel-less, or plain, and again to fishermen's seaboot stockings. The working of steering gloves, mittens, and wristlets will appeal to younger members of the family according to individual requirements. In No. 18 Ladyship leaflet appear still another style of ribbed helmet knitted, with primrose petticoat wool with gussets at the sides, whilst shaping is also effected in the neckband under the chin which is finished off by a roll collar. The same primrose petticoat wool is employed for making in ribbed crochet a soldier's sleeping cap, circular, and composed of six sections, with the edge raised upwards as a roll brim, to rest with one eye open is necessary, or allowed to drop all round for taking a perfect rest.

Boy Scouts play too great a part in the present movement not to deserve to have their wants attended to, and for this reason a well-fitting jersey, the chief garment of the juvenile uniform, is described in No. 5 Ladyship Loaflet. The measurements to suit from twelve to fourteen years of age are as follows : Length of jersey, 25 inches ; chest, 32 inches ; sleeve, 18 inches. The collar is well-turned down, and the triangular flap duly buttoned over the small breast pocket, which is either knitted or made in linen to be less clumsy. The concluding wrinkles of the instructions, explain how to modify them to fit an older boy fourteen to sixteen years old, or a younger one from ten to twelve.

THE WORK-TABLE.

TO CORRESPONDENTS.

ZIGZAG DARNING.—Use fine cotton double. On the inside of the work, 1st row, take up every other stitch.—2nd row. Take up the reverse stitch of the first row. Leave a loop of cotton at the end of each row.

COUNTRY MOUSE.—We trust the easy recipes given have been of some help in your great and unavoidable hurry for knitting your son's gloves. At the last minute space does not allow of long directions being issued on a special date.

COLLEEN.—*Address of the new Dublin needlework paper.*—The first number of the threepenny *Every Woman's Magazine of Fashion, Fancy Work, and the Home* came out last April in Dublin, where it was printed by Cahill and Co. Ltd., 40, Lower Ormond Quay. It can be obtained through your newsagents.

FLORENCE.—*Where to take lessons for working brims of lacy straw hats on a pillow.*—We have heard of this fine plaiting with straws of different thickness and glossiness, but doubt whether this fancy craft can be mastered in this country. Enquire of a straw dealer in the city. Cannot trace any instructions relating to this dainty work.

LILY O' THE VALLEY.—*Old designs suitable for tambour work, broderie Anglaise, and spangles.*—You evidently refer to the article on "Modes and Ornamentations of the Early Nineteenth Century Now Reviving," which came out in the *Queen*, Jan. 29, 1910, page 210, and contains illustrations of scalloped border, with teardrops and puckers like wolf's teeth.

KATHERINE.—*Washing woven silk. Tuition in washable painted linen.*—Procure the white hand-woven silk, 36 inches wide, from the Scottish Home Industries Association head office, 26, Great Castle-street, Oxford-circus, London, W. Lessons, linen, and paints can be had by appointment from Miss Lilian Forsyth, 175, Elm Park-mansions, Chelsea, London, S.W.

LAUREL.—*Raffia work.*—The canvas for embroidering rugs, cushions, and various items with strips of raffia can no doubt still be had from F. W. Catt and Son, 197 and 198, Sloane-street, Knightsbridge, S.W. The coloured strips and other requisites for weaving and making fancy items are occasionally available from large toy shops and in greater variety from kindergarten emporiums, such as Philip Stacey Ltd., Norwich-street, Fetter-lane, London, E.C.

FATIMA.—*Algerine work.*—Do you mean the carpet work with small patterns executed over cotton piping cord stretched the straight way of the canvas, every stitch being taken over three threads, putting the colours in as you come to them, as in raised work, and counting three stitches in width as one stitch used when copying Berlin patterns? Canvas No. 45 and cord No. 00 were used for table mats and other thick kind of work. Specimens of this work have not been seen for many years. Enquire of Berlin wool shops.

HOSPITAL WORKER.—*Colour, length, and width of mufflers.*—A good size for a serviceable muffler to be worn at the front is 12 inches wide and two yards long. Choose either navy blue, dark grey, or, better still, a deep golden shade of khaki wool not likely to fade nor soil too quickly. These mufflers are intended for very rough use, and not merely to wrap round the neck, but sometimes round the head, waist, and even to be temporarily wound round a wound as bandage. It also serves as a sling. Plain and double knitting and brioche stitch are the favourite stitches for the purposes; edge with crochet work. Fringe is not to be recommended; it is always coming in the way.

THE ELMS.—*Where to get hand-woven linens inexpensively.*—Enquire of the manageress, Miss A. Garnett, The Spinney, Fairfield, Windermere; Miss Granet, 25, Davies-street, Oxford-street, London, W., manageress of the School of Spinning and Weaving; James Winter Cartachy, Kirriemuir, developed industry of linen, weaving, and spinning, Laurencekirk, Kincardineshire; and Mrs Pepper, St. Martin's Langdale Linen Industry, Tilberthwaite, Coniston, R.S.O., Lancs. Hand-woven linen is naturally more expensive than ordinary linen, which is neither so durable nor so suitable for reproduction of antique embroideries. You have omitted to send a pseudonym. The one chosen for you we trust will be recognised by you.

ALERT HELMET.—A correspondent of the *Queen*, an expert knitter, kindly writes that the pattern of the alert helmet described in the *Queen*, Sept. 12, 1914, page 443, is very successful. She, however, points out two inadvertent errors in the figures. In the sixty-first row, where the ear openings are made: Rib 9, cast off 3, rib *37*, it should be *57*, and lower down below the ear opening *81* and not *99* stitches should be on the needle. The date given in the answer alluded to is quite correct; it refers to the illustration of a Warleigh helmet with slits for the ears which has been approved by the War Office, and which has already been copied on a large scale by knitters. Evidently to women not at the front the helmet with ears or removable openings seems the most practical cap ready to be noise and draughtproof at a minute's notice. Perhaps this temptation of sheltering the ears against a keen wind whilst on duty would be too great. Any hint or suggestion from our readers is always appreciated. The query will be attended to.

PATON'S DIRECTIONS FOR KNITTING SOLDIERS' AND SAILORS' COMFORTS.

EVERY maker of wools for knitting and crocheting has made it a point to publish sets of instructions for working with their respective specialities the principal articles of clothing required for the welfare of our men whilst on active service, either fighting, camping, laid up in hospitals, or, again, recruiting health and spirits in convalescent homes. The firm of John Paton, Son, and Co. Ltd., Alloa, has obviously contributed its share in this selection of well-tested recipes to be confidently carried out speedily by charitable amateurs, or, still better, by working women anxious to produce as quickly as possible a fair amount of these comforts so much needed at the front. To secure success in every way Paton's Alloa knitting wools, in all regular qualities and sizes, are stocked in regulation khaki shade, obtainable from all the numerous wool dealers and fancy shops keeping stores of Alloa wools, and their accompanying "Helps to Knitters," "The Universal Knitting Book," and the most comprehensive "Paton's Knitting and Crochet Book." Paton's latest penny booklet of "Directions for Knitting Soldiers' and Sailors' Comforts" contains useful recipes for working these different kinds of men's socks, and plain, ribbed, and with a particularly well-shaped leg; bag mitten, with thumb and gauntlet glove medium size, both worked on four needles; chest and neck protector, with roll collar, large size; comforter, well-shaped, to be slipped under the coat; waistcoat, in shepherd's knitting high to the throat, provided with two deep pockets; cardigan measuring 35 inches round the waist, with long sleeves and a V opening at the neck; hospital shoe, sock, slippers, the latter made in both knitting and Reversby crochet stitch; Tam o' Shanters, and four examples of Balaclava caps, with distinct crowns. To this set is added a loose sheet devoted to the latest instructions for making a helmet with ear slits as recommended by the War Office.

COMFORTS FOR THE WOUNDED.

Men's Crochet Slippers.

Two ounces of fleecy wool in any cosy, restful colour will be sufficient for these easily made slippers.

A pair of the Victor patent slipper soles, size nine or ten, simplifies the making considerably.

Use a large bone crochet hook, having the handle straight and even. Make 11 ch, turn, miss first ch, and put 1 dc into each of the others except the first, this gives 9 dc.—1st row. * 1 ch, insert the hook from right to left under the perpendicular thread on front of first dc and draw a loop through, repeat this through each dc, retaining all the loops on the needle.—2nd row. Thread over the hook and pull this loop through the first two loops on the needle, thread over the hook, and draw through next two loops and so on, two loops at a time, until all are taken off except the last.—3rd row. * Insert the hook through the perpendicular thread at extreme end of last row and draw a loop through (this gives two loops on the needle for the first stitch in order to increase one stitch at this end of the row), then raise each stitch as in the first row and increase one at the end of the row by drawing a loop through the back loop on the last stitch; there should be eleven loops on the needle.—4th row. Thread over the hook and through two loops at a time to the end of the row.* Repeat to the 10th row, then omit the increase in the 11th row, increase again in the 13th, 17th, 21st, 23rd, 25th, 27th, 29th, 33rd, and 35th rows. There should be 35 stitches in the 36th row, that is the 18th double row which forms the pattern. Raise the first 12 loops of the next row, and work a strip of 29 double rows on these 12 loops, then 8 rows more, increasing 1 at the beginning of each second row at the outside edge only. Fasten off the thread, and cut it. Fasten the thread again to the 13th stitch in the 18th double row, and form 11 loops through next 11 stitches. Work four double rows of these eleven stitches, then two more, in the sixth and eighth decreasing at each side by taking the second and third stitches from either end together and working them as one. Fasten off the thread, work the remaining 12 stitches of the 18th row to correspond with the first long strip. Place the last row beside the end of the first strip, and join by working a row of single stitches through the perpendicular stitches opposite each other, keeping the stitches on the wrong side. All round the top of the slipper work a row of single stitch, commencing at the left side, fasten the thread to the first stitch, insert the hook from the right side, and * draw a loop through, draw a loop through this loop, and pull the stitch tight; make 1 ch rather loosely *; repeat through next stitch, and so on to the

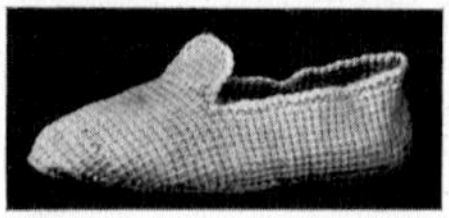

MEN'S CROCHET SLIPPERS.]

beginning of the row. Using a stout linen thread of the same colour as the wool, sew this upper to the sole immediately behind the row of piping inserted in the sole for the purpose. Fasten off the thread securely. This completes a very comfortable slipper.

Man's Bedroom Slippers.

One pair of Victor slipper soles with 2oz. of fleecy wool are required for this cosy slipper.

Using a bone crochet-hook, medium size, as the pattern must be worked closely, make 10 ch, turn.—1st row. Miss first ch, 1 dc into each of the others, this gives 9 dc.—2nd row. 1 dc into each of the first 4 dc, 3 dc into next dc, 1 dc into each of last 4 dc. Take only the portion of each stitch next the forefinger of the left hand in order to get the ribbed effect.—3rd row. * 1 ch, 1 dc into each d c with 3 dc into the centre dc of the 3 in the middle of the row. * Repeat until there are 22 rows in all. Then on the first twelve stitches work a strip eighteen rows (nine ribs),

MAN'S BEDROOM SLIPPERS.

followed by six rows more in which you increase one at the beginning of the first, third, and fifth rows. Fasten off the thread and cut it. Work a similar strip at the other side of the front, then place the two ends together and join through corresponding stitches with a row of single stitch on the wrong side. Work a row of plain dc all round the top into the end of each row and into each stitch on the point, taking up two portions of each stitch. With a stout linen thread sew this upper to the sole immediately beyond the row of piping inserted in the sole for the purpose.

RECIPES FOR KNITTING WARM GLOVES FOR OUR SAILORS AND SOLDIERS

As a general answer to several applications for directions to knit serviceable men's gloves to be sent per return, a few of the best instructions concerning these useful comforts have been gathered together, to save workers time and trouble. In this emergency it was almost useless to refer to some of the good recipes scattered in numerous books and magazines not always ready at hand. Bag-shaped gloves with thumb but no fingers and others with long gauntlets are, it appears, in special requisition. These will therefore be considered.

1. Men's gloves worked on the principle of a baby's muffatee. Here are directions for knitting this primitive handwear to suit different ideas and avoid too much sameness in the stupendous quantity required. Steering gloves answer admirably for the present purpose. The following carefully written instructions are easily grasped, and were the first given and illustrated in the *Queen* for the benefit of fishermen. The pattern worked with coarse Alloa yarn with four needles each, Nos. 12 and 13, measures at the top of the welt 4½ inches, at the wrist or beginning of glove proper, 4¼ inches; across the middle or widest part, including thumb, 6 inches; from wrist to point of glove 12½ inches; length of thumb, 6½ inches; across the lower part above the pointed end, 4½ inches. It will take 3 skeins, 2oz. each, to make two pairs of these gloves. Cast on 18 stitches on each of the three needles No. 13. Knit 36 rounds of ribbed knitting (2 plain 1 purl). Now change to pins No. 12 and knit 10 plain rounds; the larger needles give more room in the hand part, while it is desirable for the wrist to fit closely. Knit the thumb thus: Round 1—Knit 2, make 1, knit 2, make 1, knit to the end. (N.B.—To make a stitch take up the loop that goes across a stitch and knit it.) Rounds 2 and 3—Plain. Round 4—Knit 2, make 1, knit 4, make 1, knit to the end. Rounds 5 and 6—Plain. Round 7—Knit 2, make 1, knit 6, make 1, knit to end. Rounds 8 and 9—Plain. Round 10—Knit 2, make 1, knit 8, make 1, knit to end. Rounds 11 and 12—Plain. Round 13—Knit 2, make 1, knit 10, make 1, knit to end. Rounds 14 and 15—Plain. Round 16—Knit 2, make 1, knit 12, make 1, knit to end. Rounds 17 and 18—Plain. Round 19—Knit 2, make 1, knit 14, make 1, knit to end. Rounds 20 and 21—Plain. Round 22—Knit 2, make 1, knit 16, make 1, knit to end. Rounds 23 and 24—Plain. Round 25—Knit 3, make 1, knit 18, make 1, knit to the end. Round 26—Knit 3, then slip off on a bit of wool 18 stitches, and knit plain the rest of the round. Knit 34 plain rounds. Round 35—Knit 2 together, knit 4, knit 2 together, knit 4. Do the rest of the round in this manner. You will then have 15 stitches on each pin. Rounds 36, 37, 38, 39, 40, and 41—Plain. Round 42—Knit 2 together at the beginning of each needle, knitting all the rest of stitches plain. Rounds 43, 44, 45, 46, 47, 48, 49, and 50—Plain. Round 51—Knit 2 together, and continue this throughout the round. This will leave 7 stitches on each needle. Round 52—Plain. Round 53—Knit 2 together, and continue this throughout the round. Knit the odd stitch plain at the end. Round 54—Plain. Break off the wool, leaving an end 6 inches long, with which thread a coarse wool needle. On this needle slip off the stitches from the first needle, and draw the wool through them. Do this with the remaining stitches, and draw them up tightly, to close the mitten. Run your wool round through the stitches a second time, then pass the needle to the inside of the mitten, and fasten off by darning up and down three or four lines, as it ought to be made very secure. For the thumb, take up the 18 stitches from the bit of wool, and pick up three or four more in the gap left between the last stitch and the first.

Left: Featured in *The Queen* on 24 October 1914, this pattern for crocheted slippers was ideal for convalescent soldiers.

Right: A combined muffler and sleeping hood for soldiers at the front made – ideally – in fleecy, khaki wool with a bone crochet hook, from *The Queen*, 31 October 1914.

ZITA.—*Territorial colours.*—Consult Mrs Evershed, Embroidery Studio, 59, South Molton-street, London, W. She will give you every satisfaction for banners, whether entirely worked or prepared to be embroidered by you, with a design made according to your clear directions.

COUNTRY LASS.—*What to do with seeds available in large quantities.*—Some may be introduced in embroidery, marqueterie, or for decorating rustic frames or jars. For the latter select prettily shaped vases, smear them with strong gum. When perfectly dry, paint over with Aspinal enamel, slightly sprinkling with gold or silver dust. Use some of the largest seed as petals of flowers, to which add painted leaves. Stars outlined with chalk are also effectively treated in this way. And, again, mats, chains, and bracelets made of threaded seeds are fashionable.

NANARISMA.—*A recipe wanted for colouring ornamental grass and moss permanently.*—For dark green take two parts of boiling water, 1oz. alum, and ½oz. dissolved indigo carmine. Plunge the moss or grass into the mixture, shake off the liquid, and dry in a shady place, or in winter by means of fire heat. Use aniline dyes for other colours. This recipe was given in a paper full of practical hints on the best methods of drying flowers to present a uniform flat surface or to retain their natural form. Refer to *Queen*, Nov. 30, 1912, page 1000.

NORTHERN LIGHTS.—*Directions wanted for making a nightingale worked jacket out of a length of material without any cutting.*—

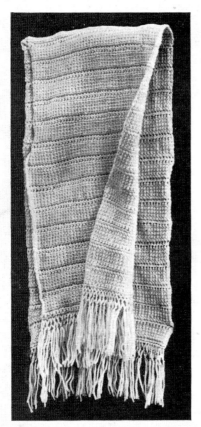

MUFFLER AND SLEEPING HOOD COMBINED.

COMFORTS FOR THE WOUNDED.
Muffler and Sleeping Hood Combined.

THREE-QUARTERS of a pound of khaki fleecy wool with a b crochet hook are required for this useful article.

The muffler is about two yards long and half a yard w When used as a sleeping hood there are patent fasteners on centre at each side, which close the edges in order to form hood. By pulling the ends the hood can be immediately unde and resolves itself into the muffler again.

Alternate rows of long-connected trebles and dc form muffler. Make a half-yard length of ch stitches, turn and w the first row of dc into these chs, making 1 ch at the begin of every row of dc.—2nd row (the "long connected trs"), draw a loop through the fourth, third, second, and first ch retain them on the needle, draw a loop through next dc, you h now six loops on the needle, thread over the hook and thro next two loops on the needle, thread over the hook and thro next two, and so on, working off two at a time until the six finished. * Look back on this stitch and you will see h horizontal threads crossing it. Raise a loop through each these four bars and retain them on the needle, draw a l through next dc, you have again six loops on the begin which you work off as before * repeat to the end of the n The next and each succeeding alternate row is dc worked thro both portions of the top stitch. Finish with a row of dc.

For the fringe you wind the thread around a piece of ca board 8 inches deep. Cut one end, then take the threads one one, fold in two, draw the loop through the top of a dc w the crochet hook, insert the two ends through the loop and dr up closely. In this way fringe each dc at both ends. Then in the fringe in the usual way for two rows.

Six patent fasteners are sewn near the edge at one side af folding the muffler in two to get the centre, placing correspond halves of the fasteners at the end of the dc rows about 1½ inch from the extreme edge. The front edge is then rolled back make the hood fit the head comfortably.

USEFUL HINTS FOR KNITTERS OF SOCKS.

A RECENT CORRESPONDENT from the front says he came across a place where the soldiers had just been snatching a few moments' rest and changing their socks. Of course they had thrown away the socks they had taken off, and a great number were lying over the place. Out of curiosity the correspondent examined some of them, and found that i all cases the leg and heel were intact, but that part of the sole that comes under the ball of the foot and the toe part were destroyed.

This fact shows that the greatest wear is on the upper half of the foot, and the best way to remedy this is to have this portion of the sock double, *not* knitted with a double thread, but with a knitted lining to this portion. If the sock be knitted with four-ply fingering, finish the toe part for half the length of the entire foot, with three-ply wool of the same colour as the sock, or white, raise every stitch on the edge of the 'old, and repeat the stitches in this part of the sock to the toe, finishing off as in the toe of the sock. The result is a knitted lining to that part which requires strengthening,

A MAN'S CROCHETED GLOVE.

and the sock will not only be more lasting, but warmer and more comfortable than that strengthened by doubling the thread.

Man's Crocheted Glove.

The crocheted glove is more serviceable than a knitted one, as well as being so much easier to make.

Two and a half ounces of wool will be required, and a No. 1 steel crochet hook.

Commence with 29 ch, turn, miss 1 ch, and work a dc into each of the other 28 ch, turn with 1 ch and work fifty rows of ribbing by putting a dc into that portion of each of the dc that lies next the forefinger of the left hand. Close the two ends by a row of single stitches through corresponding stitches in the first and last rows.

At the upper side of this wrist part put a dc into the end of every row and one into the stitch between the ribs. This gives 75 stitches. Work 16 rows.

Next row : 1 dc into each of 43 dc, 5 ch, turn these over to the 24th dc and put a dc into it, continue working round on the 20 dc and the 6 ch (putting a dc into each of them), and form 18 rows of 26 stitches each, then decrease after every third dc by taking a loop through each of the 2 dc and working of the two loops with that on the needle at the same time. Close the top of the finger with a few tight single stitches and cut off the thread. Work the end of the thread back through a few of the stitches. Fasten the thread to the first of the 6 ch at the base of the thumb and continue work-

ing round and round for 18 rows. There should be 61 stitches.

Work the next row as far as the two stitches in a line with the beginning of the thumb, on these and the following 16

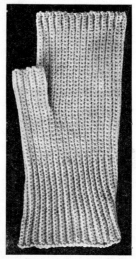

A CROCHET MITTEN.

stitches, that is, 18 in all, commence the forefinger, make 6 ch and join round to the first of the 18, working dc into each stitch for 21 rows, then decreasing as for the thumb. Finish the point in the same way. The second finger is commenced, 8th dc before the first on the front. Put a dc into each of these, then a dc through each of the six chain raised between this finger and the first, put a dc through each of the next 7 dc on the back, make 6 ch, and join round to the first of the 8 dc on the front. Work 24 rows before decreasing as before.

For the third finger take 5 dc preceding the second on the front, the six between the second and third fingers, five on the back, and make 6 ch, then work round as before for 22 rows, and decrease as before. The fourth finger is worked on the remaining 12, and the six raised on the 6 ch after the third finger, 18 stitches in all, on which 15 rows are worked, then decrease.

This being the side of the glove on which the fastenings were made is the wrong side.

Man's Crochet Mitten.

Required, 2oz. of navy 4-ply fingering, and a No. 1 steel crochet hook.

Make 65 ch, turn, miss first ch and put 1 dc into each of the others for 64 dc, turn, 1 ch. *1 dc into each of the first 5 dc, taking only that portion of each that lies next the forefinger of the left hand, 34 dc into next 34, taking up both of the top portions, 25 into the last 25, taking only that portion next the forefinger of the left hand ; turn with 1 ch, 25 dc into last 25, taking only one portion as before, 34 dc into next 34, taking both portions, 5 dc into next 5 taking only 1 portion* ; repeat for 25 rows from the beginning.

In the 26th row work as far as the 12th stitch beyond the ribbing at the wrist part, make 14 ch, turn, miss the first ch, and put a dc into each of the others. Continue down to the end of the row, turn, 1 ch as before, and work the pattern on this piece, putting the 5 stitches of ribbing at the top of the thumb part, for 14 rows.

Leave the gauntlet part for the present, and fasten a long piece of the thread to the top of the first row on the thumb, work the dc into the 12 on the thumb, and continue up to the top of the band part; work 4 rows like this, then 1 row on the 12 in the thumb, fasten the thread, and cut it off. Then resume from the part left off, and work to the top for 26 rows more. Close the side with a row of single stitch. Finish the edges with 2 ch, 1 single into the middle of every rib.

To Wash Knitted Woollen Gloves.

Make a very warm soapy lather, and in another basin prepare the rinsing water of the same temperature, having a large teaspoonful of glycerine mixed in it. Immerse the gloves in the soapy water, do not rub them, but squeeze the water through several times, then squeeze out as much as

Left: Crocheted gloves and mittens for soldiers and sailors from *The Queen*, 14 November 1914.

Right: The Graphic's 21 November 1914 issue printed instructions on how to make mittens from old socks and stockings, an idea devised by Dr George C. Cathcart of Harley Street for supplying the London Scottish Regiment in which he had long served.

Far right: Crochet mitten with wrist gauntlets for extra protection, from *The Queen*, 12 December 1914.

TO MAKE MITTENS FROM SOCKS

Dr. George C. Cathcart, of 52, Harley Street, has hit on an ingenious plan for supplying the London Scottish (in which he long served) with mittens. He does so by utilising old socks and stockings.

Cut the sock or stocking across as close to the heel as possible, at the line A B, and bind or turn in the edge, sewing it over neatly and firmly. If the sock be hand-knitted the wool may be unravelled for a row or two and the stitches picked up on a crochet hook and finished off with a row of single crochet.

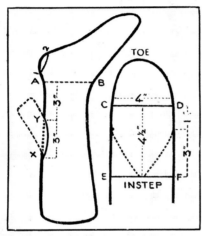

The thumb is made from the front piece of the foot of the sock, and should be 4½ to 5 inches long to allow for finishing off the top. Finish off edge as above, fold the piece lengthwise, and sew the two edges for 1in. from the finished top firmly together. Round off the remaining 3in. to the shape of the thumb of a glove. Make a slit 3in. long in the back of the sock, starting from X, 6in. from the cut edge and carrying it to Y 3in. from that edge. To set in the thumb, turn the stocking leg inside out, and slip the thumb right side out into the slit, so that the edges of the thumb lie against the edges of the slit. Sew firmly, taking care that the edges are caught up and cannot unravel.

If ladies' thin socks or men's thin socks be used there must be two socks to each mitten, and they must be sewn very carefully together. If one thin stocking be used it should be doubled in for nine inches before setting in the thumb. If the sock be loosely woven it is better to make the distance from A to X 4 or 5in. instead of 3in., and turn down the edge for an inch or two in order to make a double piece along the edge, which prevents the edge stretching unduly and makes it cling more closely to the fingers. To make the mittens without thumbs, make a slit in the point of the heel, large enough to put a man's thumb through, at the Nos. 1 and 2, and sew all round with a buttonhole stitch. Then cut off the front of the sock 4 or 5in. from the thumb hole and finish as before. In some cases the socks could be used as gloves without fingers by making the thumb hole as above, and turning in the toe from side to side (not from back to front) and sewing it to the part that is going to be at the back of the fingers, then sew over the top edges.

A CROCHET MITTEN.
Gauntlet Wrist and Hand in One.

NINETY chain, turn 2 chain, miss 1, then 36 short treble, then 12 double crochet, then 42 treble, turn 3 loose chain, miss 1, or repeat treble on treble, double crochet on double crochet, and short treble on short treble 34 runs. All stitches to be worked into the back to make it ribbed. Join hand at top 16 stitches and break off.

Thumb.—22 chain turn.—1st row. 2 *tight* chain, miss 1, 22 double crochet, counting the first 2 chain as 1 turn.—2nd row. No chain, 22 d.c., turn.—3rd row. 2 chain, miss 1, 20 d.c., missing last two stitches, turn.—4th row. Miss 2, 18 d.c., turn.—5th row. 2 chain, miss 1, 17 d.c., turn.—6th row. Miss 1, 16 d.c.—7th row. 2 chain, miss 1, 14 d.c.—8th row. Miss 1, 13 d. crochet.—9th row. 2 chain, miss 1, 12 d.c.—10th row. 2 chain, miss 1, 11 d.c.—11th row. 2 chain, miss 1, 11 d.c., and 3 chain at end to increase turn, miss 1 chain, and d.c. the row, and repeat second half of thumb; leave 3¾ yards of wool to join thumb, wrist, and gauntlet after thumb is inserted.

Thumb is inserted about 3 stitches from wrist, and double crochet all round very neatly, then join thumb, wrist, and gauntlet right down. If thick wool is used, 30 or 32 runs will be enough for the mitten. The thumb is worked about the same in all wools. Four ounces of *good* wool required, to be worked very tightly and evenly with a very *small* straight hook. In turning rows at top of hand keep the 2 chain *tight*; in turning rows at gauntlet end keep the 3 chain *loose*. The short treble is: Wool over hook as for ordinary treble; insert the hook in the chain, draw wool through, wool over hook, and draw through all the loops on the hook at once.

THESE WRAPS give extra protection where it is most needed, and as the flaps extend across the whole chest there is no opening down the front. The revers can be closed or open according to the weather. They are very simple in their construction and easy to work, being made in two strips, and having a short seam under each arm and a longer one down the back. The neck forms a point at the back and is straight under the chin. They reach about 2 inches below the waist, a cord being used to keep the flaps in their place. There are two sizes, for small and large women.

The implements and materials to be used are as follows : Two pins size 5, 6oz. or 7oz. of five-ply fingering or of wheeling yarn. To make smaller ones for children use pins and yarn one size finer.

Cast on 26 or 30 stitches. Slip the first stitch and knit the last in each row, and work the rest in huckaback pattern as follows : Rows 1 and 2. Knit 2, purl 2 ; repeat.—Rows 3 and 4. Purl 2, knit 2 ; repeat.

Work 120 or 130 of these rows. At the end of the last of them cast on 18 or 22 more stitches, making 44 or 52 in all. Continue the pattern, keeping it correct where the new stitches begin. Work 100 or 110 more rows, so forming the chest flap, and making 220 or 240 rows in all, and cast off.

Work another piece with the following difference : Cast on the new stitches at the end of the row *before* the last one, so making the flap on the opposite side of the work to which it is in the first piece ; in the next row knit the new stitches and finish the row in the pattern, continue as before directed, and cast off.

To make this up, put one piece on the other, both flaps at one side, and the wrong sides out. Begin to sew the back seam 2 or 3 inches from the narrow end, at the flap side, to within the same length of the flaps ; this will leave a point

THE DOUBLE-BREASTED WRAP.

at the back of the neck. Open the work and fold it in half across its length ; then sew the side seams, beginning at the same distance from the end of the strip as in the back, leaving plenty for the armholes. Work a row of crochet scallops along the edge of both fronts, the neck, and the armholes, keeping the right side of the work outside. Make a cord about a yard and a half long, twisted fourfold or a crochet chain two or three fold, in the wrap yarn, and add large tassels or balls securely fastened on. Sew the cord to the waist on the back seam, the portion under the right arm being the longer, so that the tassels may hang just in front of the left arm.

These wraps can be worked in one colour only, or in two colours, or in two shades of one colour, or in white and coloured, the stripes being the same or different widths ; in the last three cases the rever does not look so well turned down, as the back of the new colour stitches show plainly. If these stripes are worked in a pattern all the stitches must be knitted in each first row of the stripes. Any small design of two or three stitches and two, four or six rows to a pattern can be used, except brioche, a well-known one, which contracts much in its width. If plain knitting is used throughout, so making ridges, about twenty to thirty more rows will be needed in each part of the strip, as ridges contract the work in its length ; also, making a thicker garment, it may be well to use pins one size larger.

These wraps made large enough in thick and strong yarn would doubtless be much appreciated as extra waistcoats by men exposed to severe weather.

HENRIETTA WARLEIGH COPTHORNE.

Left: Photograph and accompanying pattern for a knitted, double-breasted wrap made in thick, strong yarn and designed by Henrietta Warleigh in *The Queen* magazine, 30 January 1915. The magazine expresses that they 'would doubtless be much appreciated as extra waistcoats by men exposed to severe weather'.

Right: The Warleigh Smoking Cap designed by Henrietta Warleigh and published in *The Queen* magazine in 1915. It was designed to be worn by convalescent soldiers and sailors, though why exactly they needed a woolly hat in which to smoke is not explained.

THE WARLEIGH SMOKING CAP.

IT IS WELL KNOWN that smoking has a soothing effect and helps to while away many hours of weakness and pain. These caps will therefore be useful to those of our

THE WARLEIGH SMOKING CAP.

naval and military friends who are filling hospitals and homes after a noble performance of duty. Prevention being better than cure, they will also ward off colds, which so often lead to serious illness, especially in the case of invalids who are very open to a relapse. One can easily be made in two or three days.

The dashes enclose the nine stitches which form the handsome plait which encircles the head, each of its three strands being three stitches wide. R. and L. H. P. mean right and left hand pins.

Things required: two pins size 4, 2oz. of double Berlin, or any other wool of the same size.

Cast on 6, 9, and 15 = 30 stitches.

Row 1. Knit 30.

Rows 2, 4, 6, and 8. Knit 15—purl 9—knit 6.

Row 3. Knit 6—make the first and second strands change places thus: Slip the 6 stitches off the L. H. P., pick up the second strand with the R. H. P., keep it at the back, then pick up the first strand with the L. H. P., keep it in front, and return the second strand to the L. H. P., so making them cross each other; do this without twisting the stitches. The middle strand is always to be kept at the back, and put into each side space alternately. Knit the 6 stitches in the new order, knit 3, which form the third strand—knit 15.

Row 5. Knit 30.

Row 7. Knit 6—knit 3, which form the first strand, then make the second and third strands change places, thus: Slip the 6 stitches off the L. H. P., pick up the third strand with the R. H. P., keep it in front, then pick up the second strand, that is, the middle one, with the L. H. P., keep it at the back, and return the third strand to the L. H. P., so making them cross each other. Knit the 6 stitches in the new order –knit 15.

Work these 8 rows 14 more times, then work to the end of the fifth row, cast off double with the cast-on stitches, the inside of the cap facing the worker. Gather the edge of the wide margin with stitches 4 ridges long, using the wool double, draw it up as tight as possible, so making 8 large tapering flutes. If preferred a button, tuft, or tassel can be put here as a finish. Many persons think this cap looks better without them.

There will be 15½ patterns of eight rows—that is, 4 ridges each, making 124 rows, 62 ridges. It will be a help to mark the number of rows by putting a long stitch of white cotton after every fourth ridge as the work grows; this will also prevent any parts of the plait being too long. Do this in the narrow margin.

For a small cap for children use pins 7 and 1½oz. of Alloa wheeling, the best quality. A row of large scallops along the edge of the narrow margin is an improvement for women and children.

The margins can be worked in the following pattern. In this case they should be 5 and 17 stitches wide. Slip the first stitch and knit the last one in each row to make an even edge.

Huckaback, Size 2.

Rows 1 and 2. Knit 2, purl 2.—Rows 3 and 4. Purl 2, knit 2.

Cast off after 15 patterns have been worked, as it rather expands the knitting, so making the cap a little larger than the plain knitting does.   HENRIETTA WARLEIGH.

The M. I. K.
(Man in Khaki)
SOCK MEASURE or SOCK-KNITTER'S HELP.

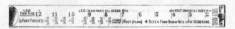

Knitting made easy by using the M.I.K. Tape and following the Directions given. The M.I.K. Tape enables amateurs readily to acquire quickness in Sock knitting. The measure gauge saves much time in counting, and ensures each sock being exactly alike.

SEPARATELY BOXED.   Each (advertised).

Knitting made easy by using The M.I.K. Tape and following the

DIRECTIONS.

No. 13 Needles : 4-ply super-fingering or wheeling worsted.
Cast on 60 stitches.

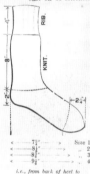

i.e., from back of heel to decrease of toe

Work, in rib of knit 2 and purl 2, for 32 rounds = 4 in.

Work 8 inches in plain knitting with no shaping = 12 in. from top, making a seam stitch all down the leg, *i.e.*, one stitch to be knitted purl and plain alternately.

For the heel, put 31 stitches on the 1st needle, 15 on the 2nd and 14 on the 3rd.

On the 31 stitches knit, alternately plain and purl, 26 rows, always slipping the first stitch and continuing the seam stitch. The 27th row (x) knit plain to within 3 of seam stitch, knit 2 together, knit 1 plain, seam stitch, knit 1 plain, knit 2 together and finish row plain. The 28th row purl. Repeat from (x). This leaves 27 stitches on the needle. The seam stitch now ceases, but slipping the 1st stitches continues.

To turn the heel, (x) knit plain to 2 beyond the seam stitch, knit 2 together, turn, purl to 2 beyond the seam stitch, purl 2 together, turn and repeat from (x) till there are 7 on the needle.

For the instep, follow on with the same needle and pick up and knit the 14 stitches on the side of the heel. Knit on to the 2nd needle the 15 and the 14 left for the instep when beginning the heel. Then, with the 3rd needle, pick up and knit the 14 stitches on the other side of the heel, at the end adding 3 from the 1st needle. In the next row increase 4 on each heel needle. This is done by raising an extra stitch between every 3rd or 4th stitch.

Next row plain, then begin the decreasings : knit the 3rd and 4th stitches together from the end of the 1st needle, and on the 3rd needle, knit 2, slip 1, knit 1, pass the slipped stitch over the knitted. Do this in every third round until there are 15 stitches on each of the 1st and 3rd needles. Knit without shaping until the work measures from the heel : —

Size 1. 7¾ in., making full length of foot + toe 2¼ in. = 10 in.
 ,, 2. 8¼ in., ,,   ,,   ,,   = 10½ in.
 ,, 3. 8¾ in., ,,   ,,   ,,   = 11 in.
 ,, 4. 9¼ in., ,,   ,,   ,,   = 11½ in.

For the toe, (x) knit to the last 3 stitches on the 1st needle, knit 2 together, knit 1 : on the instep needle, knit 1, slip 1, knit 1, pass the slipped stitch over the knitted, knit to the last 3 stitches on the needle, knit 2 together, knit 1 : on the 3rd needle, knit 1, slip 1, knit 1, pass the slipped stitch over the knitted, knit to the end of the needle.

Knit 1 round plain.

Repeat from (x) until the toe is reduced to 24 stitches. Divide these on 2 needles.

Break off the wool, leaving about half a yard, with which thread a wool needle. Hold with this at the back, and (x) insert it in the 1st stitch of the front needle as if for plain knitting, take off the stitch, and insert again as if for purling, draw wool through but leave the 2nd stitch on the knitting needle. Then on the back needle take off the 1st stitch as if for purling, insert again as if for plain knitting and draw the wool through, but leave the stitch on the needle. Repeat from (x) till all the stitches are worked off ; pull the wool through the last stitch and run in the end to make firm.

The simple formula for the above method of taking off the toe is as follows:—
Front Needle—From you, take off. To you, don't take off.
Back Needle—To you, take off. From you, don't take off.

THE CUMBERLAND MITTEN.
Specially Designed for the Use of Soldiers at the Front.

The following instructions are for knitted mittens which have been arrived at after several experiments. The mitten when submitted to soldiers who had seen much active service were received with unanimous approval. A large number of these mittens were made last winter and sent out to the trenches, and have met with the highest commendation.

No. 1 Illustration shows the mitten as worn when freedom is desired for the fingers and thumb, and No. 2 with the mitten drawn down over the thumb and fingers, giving greater warmth when freedom is not necessary. One can let me impress upon my readers, namely, when the mittens have been completed, turn back the portions as shewn in illustration No. 2, and tack the pair together at the thumb, the fingers, and at the wrist, so that when a soldier receives them he may at once see how they are to be worn. Of his own initiative he will turn them down as in illustration No. 2 when the occasion requires. Also, and let this be writ large in a knitter's memory, tack them together with white cotton, not wool, or the soldier will be as likely to cut the mitten as the tacking—and let it be done securely.

This mitten has the further advantage of being easily knitted. I knit the hand portion in khaki, and, as this colour is more difficult to procure than others, I make the leg and toe portion in any other colour providing it is suitable.

Instructions.—Cast on 36 loops. Knit 28 ribs. Knit 18 loops, and then cast on 10 loops for the thumb on the needle upon which you have just knitted the 18. Knit back to the wrist, but do not knit the last loop. Knit to the end of the 10 loops. Then knit back to the wrist, leaving 2 loops unknitted. Then knit to the end of the 10 loops, then back to the wrist, leaving 3 loops. Repeat until you have 10 unknitted loops. Now knit up the remaining 18 loops (these 18 loops are on the short needle in No. 3 illustration). Then knit 11 ribs, or more should a wider mitten be desired.

Sew up the thumb and the hand portion of the mitten. Then take up 44 loops at the wrist, and knit 2 and purl 2 for about 4 inches.

Needles, 10 bell gauge. Wool, Alloa.

AUGUSTA A. VARTY-SMITH.

FIG. 1.

FIG. 2.

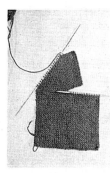
FIG. 3.

WRISTLET WITH THUMB HOLE
(See cut page 7)

Materials: 1 skein Scotch yarn, gray, khaki, or blue.

Cast on 60 stitches (20 on each of 3 needles);

Knit 2, purl 2 for 10 inches;

Knit back and forth for 1½ inches for thumb hole, then knit around for 1 inch more.

Bind off loosely.

SQUARES FOR AFGHANS

Materials: Use any scraps of wool. If wool is thin, knit double.

Make 8 inches square. 60 squares make a good-sized afghan—10 squares long and 6 squares wide.

HELMET No. 1

Materials: 1½ skeins Scotch yarn, gray, khaki, or blue. Needles: 4 No. 4 double-pointed amber.

Cast on 100 stitches, using 2 needles; knit 2, purl 2, for 7 inches.

Leave 26 on pin and knit 74 plain for 6 inches;

Bind off 26 at each end and knit 22 for 6 inches;

Sew up 2 sides and pick up all around for the face 90 to 100 stitches on 3 needles;

Knit 2, purl 2 for 1½ inches;

Bind off loosely.

HELMET, No. 2

Materials: 1½ skeins Scotch yarn, gray, khaki, or blue. Needles: 4 No. 12 steel and 4 No. 4 amber, double points.

Cast on 56 stitches on No. 4 amber needles. Knit backward and forward for about 5 inches. This forms the cape on one side. Make a second piece just like the first one for the second cape. Divide the stitches to form the neck on 3 amber needles, joining as in making a stocking. Knit 2 and purl 2 for about 3 or 4 inches.

Leave 32 stitches in the middle of the front cape for the face, slip onto safety pin. Knit the remaining stitches (84) on the amber needles; knit backward and forward, as in the cape, for 45 ridges (over and back making 1 ridge).

Bind off 26 stitches on each side of the 84. Knit the 32 stitches left on the needle for 26 ridges. Sew these 26 ridges to the sides. On the No. 12 steel needles knit up all the stitches around the face of the hood, add those left on the safety pin at the neck. Knit 2 and purl 2 for 20 rows. This forms the face.

Bind off on right side.

8

9

KNITTED HELMET (WITH CAPE PIECES)

BY MARJORY TILLOTSON.

MATERIALS REQUIRED.—4 ozs. J. & J. BALDWIN'S "WHITE HEATHER" Fleecy Wool, four No. 8 Celluloid Knitting Needles, pointed at each end.

Cast 30 stitches on one needle.

Knit plain, and increase once at the beginning of each row until 50 stitches are on the needle.

Knit 5 more inches in plain knitting.

Leave this piece and knit a second piece exactly like it.

Now place the two pieces together, dividing the stitches on to three needles. Take a fourth needle and work in rounds, in ribbing of knit 2 and purl 2, for 6 inches.

Cast off 24 stitches **over the centre of one of the cape pieces,** to make the opening for the face.

Work backwards and forwards (in the rib) for 2 inches.

Cast on 24 stitches again, over the opening, and join up the round.

Work 4 more inches in the rib.

Finish the cap in plain knitting as follows :—

1st round.—Knit each 19th and 20th stitches together.

2nd round.—Knit plain with no shaping.

3rd round.—Knit each 18th and 19th stitches together.

Repeat the 2nd round.

5th round.—Knit each 17th and 18th stitches together.

6th round.—Knit each 16th and 17th stitches together.

Continue in this manner, decreasing each round, until only 25 stitches remain.

Run a thread through these and fasten off securely.

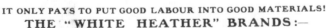

Pattern for a knitted helmet with cape pieces by Marjory Tillotson, published in a Baldwin's knitting booklet.

RELIEF WORK

DIRECTIONS FOR KNITTING ARTICLES SUITABLE
FOR THE ARMY, NAVY AND EUROPEAN SUFFERERS

SOCKS	HELMETS
MITTENS	WRISTERS
BANDS	MUFFLERS
HOSPITAL STOCKINGS	

The colors most suitable for making above both for hospital purposes as well as for men engaged in active service, are the grey, brown and olive-drab mixtures for the Army and dark blues for the Navy.

Men's Socks

MATERIAL
Columbia Spanish Knitting Yarn
2 hanks
or Columbia Inverness Wool
3 hanks
5 Steel Knitting Needles No. 13

Cast on 80 stitches (divided on 4 needles having 20 stitches on each needle) knit 2, purl 2, for 4 inches. Then knit plain. Make 1 seam stitch, knit until sock measures 7 inches. Then decrease 1 stitch each side of seam by knitting 2 together. Repeat these 5 times with 5 rows plain between each decreasing. Knit plain until sock measures 10½ inches.

Now begin the heel. Use the 2 needles on each side of the seam for the heel, slip 3 stitches from the front needles onto the back needles having 18 stitches on each needle. Now work back and forth on 2 back needles omitting the seam stitch. Knit 1 row, purl 1 row until heel measures 3 inches. Slip stitches on the 1 needle with wrong side toward you. Purl 24 stitches, purl the 25th and the 26th stitch together turn * slip 1 stitch, knit 12 stitches not counting the slip stitch knit 13th and 14th stitch together turn slip 1st stitch. Purl 12 stitches, purl 13th and 14th. Repeat from * until all stitches are worked off having the 14th center stitch left. Now divide on the 2 needles having 7 stitches on each needle. Pick up 15 stitches on each side of heel, kint 3 rows plain divide stitches, leaving 17 stitches on each one of the 2 front needles and 22 stitches on back needles. Now decrease 1 stitch on the first back needle. Knit 1, knit 2 together, knit to end of needle. Knit 2nd back needle within 3 stitches, knit 2 together knit 1 row plain decrease the same way with 1 plain row between it until 17 stitches are left. Knit plain until foot measures 8 inches. Now decrease 1 stitch at each end of needle every other row until 7 stitches are left on each needle. Then decrease every row until all the stitches are taken off.

There are 32 different combinations in this stock to select from.

CAP AND SCARF COMBINED (IN CROCHET)

MATERIALS REQUIRED.—9 ozs. J. & J. BALDWIN'S "WHITE HEATHER" Fleecy Wool, a No. 7 Crochet Hook.

Commence with 38 ch.

Work backwards and forwards in d.c., always taking up both threads and turning with 2 ch., until 36 inches are completed. Fasten off.

Work a second piece like the above.

Place the two pieces together, letting an end of one piece overlap an end of the other piece for about 10 inches. Sew round the two ends and one of the open sides, thus forming the cap part of the scarf.

Left: 'Cap and scarf combined' – a particularly snug combination.

Right: A little light relief from knitting socks, this crochet military uniform for a doll appeared in *The Needlworker* magazine in March 1915.

Doll Dressed in Crochet as Soldier

The illustration is a Doll 10 inches high.

Required : about 2 ounces of " Peacock " Khaki Fingering, 1 bone crochet hook, small leather strap, small quantity of Cream Star Sylko, 1 dozen gilt buttons and 4 small buttons.

For Knickers.

Make 17 ch., join round, 1 d.c. into each ch.

2nd row.—3 ch., 1 tr. into each of 16 sts.

3rd row.—2 tr. into each st.

4th row.—1 tr. into each st.

5th row.—* 1 tr. into st., 1 tr. into two next sts. together ; repeat from *.

6th and 7th rows.— 1 tr. into each st. Make the other leg the same.

Now take one leg and work 1 tr. into 12th st., 1 tr. into next 11 sts., then work on next leg 1 tr. into every st. and round on first leg where you commenced the row.

2nd row.—1 tr. into st., 1 tr. into two next sts. together and repeat.

3rd row.—1 tr. into each st., then fasten off.

For Coat.

Back.—Make 23 ch., 1 tr. into 4th and every following ch.

2nd row.—1 tr. into each st.

3rd and 4th rows.— Like 2nd row.

5th row.—3 ch., 1 tr. into 2 sts. together, 1 tr. into each st. until last two, 1 tr. into both these together.

6th row.—Like 5th row.

7th row.—1 tr. into each st.

8th row.—2 tr. into first and last sts., 1 tr. into other sts.

9th row.—2 tr. into first st., 1 tr. into 5

next sts., 1 d.c. into 7 sts., 1 tr. into 5 sts., 2 tr. into next.

10th row.—2 tr. into first st., 1 into 4 sts., 1 d.c. into 11 sts., 1 tr. into 4 sts., 2 tr. into last. Fasten off.

For Front.—Make 13 ch.

1 tr. into fourth and following sts.

2nd, 3rd and 4th rows.—1 tr. into each st.

5th row.—3 ch., 1 tr. into 2 sts. together, 1 tr. into each of following sts.

6th row.—1 tr. into each st., 1 in 2 last sts. together.

7th row.—1 tr. into each st.

8th row.—Like 7th row.

9th row.—2 tr. into first st., 1 tr. into 4 sts., 1 d.c. into 2 sts.

10th row.—1 d.c. into 4 sts., 1 tr. into 3 sts., 2 tr. into last st.

Make second front like first.

Sew up and work one row of tr. round top.

For Sleeve.

Make 18 ch., 1 tr. into fourth and following sts.

2nd row.—2 tr. into first and last sts., 1 tr. into other sts.

3rd row.—1 tr. into each st.

4th row.—2 tr. into first and last st., 1 tr. into others.

5th row.—1 d.c. into 4 sts., 1 tr. into 12 sts., 1 d.c. into 4 sts.

6th row.—6 d.c., 7 tr., 6 d.c.

Work a row of d.c. round cuff. Make both sleeves alike and sew into coat.

Arm Straps.

Join wool to front of sleeve and work 6 tr. along top, turn, and work 5 tr. on these 6 tr., then turn again and work 4 tr., and last row 3 tr.

HELMET (WITH CAPE PIECES)

By MARJORY TILLOTSON

❡ **War Office Experts** do not recommend apertures for the ears, the latter particularly requiring protection in cold weather.

MATERIALS REQUIRED.—4½ ozs. (1½ Cuts) J. & J. BALDWIN'S 3 ply "White Heather" Wheeling. Five No. 8 Celluloid Knitting Needles.
(BEEHIVE DOUBLE KNITTING WOOL may be used as an alternative, following the same instructions).

Cast on 30 stitches.

Knit plain, and increase once at the beginning of each row until 50 stitches are on the needle.

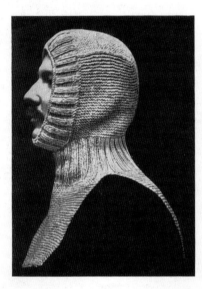

Knit 5 more inches in plain knitting.

Leave this piece on the needle and knit a second piece exactly like it.

Now place the two pieces together dividing the stitches on to three needles. Take a fourth needle and work in rounds, in ribbing of knit 2 and purl 2, for 4 inches.

Slip the 20 stitches from the centre of one of the Cape pieces on to a thread and leave these for the opening for the face. Knit plain backwards and forwards on the remaining stitches for 60 rows, always slipping the first stitch.

For the shaping at the top of the helmet, knit 53, slip 1, knit 1, pass the slipped stitch over the knitted, turn, * knit 28, slip 1, knit 1, pass the slipped stitch over the knitted, turn, repeat from * until all the stitches are worked in, leaving the 29 stitches on the needle. Break off the wool and commence again where the 20 stitches were left on the thread. Knit them in the rib as before; take another needle, follow on and, working in rib of knit 2 and purl 2 all round the face, knit up 30 stitches along the edge of the 60 plain rows; with a third needle knit across the 29 stitches at the top of the face and knit 2 of the stitches together to make the rib fit in exactly; then with a fourth needle knit up 30 stitches at the other side of the face.

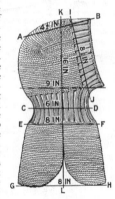

Work 16 rounds in rib of knit 2 and purl 2.

Cast off.

3

Precise instruction for a knitted helmet with cape by Marjory Tillotson in a Baldwin's knitting leaflet. The garment covers much of the head, neck and chest, leaving the face only just visible.

PLAIN HELMET (or BALACLAVA CAP)

MATERIALS REQUIRED.—4 ozs. (1 Cut) J & J. BALDWIN'S "White Heather" Wheeling (or "Beehive" Double Knitting Wool), Four No. 8 Celluloid Knitting Needles.

Cast on 100 stitches, 36 on to one needle and 32 on to each of the other two needles.

Work, in rounds of ribbing (knit 2 and purl 2), until the fabric measures 12 inches.
Cast off 24 stitches loosely to make the opening for the face.

Work backwards and forwards (in the rib) for 2 inches. Cast on 24 stitches again and join up the round. Work 4 more inches in the rib.

Finish the cap in plain knitting and decrease as follows :

1st round. — Knit each 19th and 20th stitch together.

Knit 1 round plain.

3rd round. — Knit each 18th and 19th stitch together.

Knit 1 round plain.

5th round. — Knit each 17th and 18th stitch together.

Knit 1 round plain.

Decrease in this manner until only 25 stitches remain. Run a thread through these and fasten off securely.   M.T.

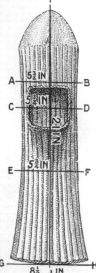

SLEEPING CAP

MATERIALS REQUIRED :—
2½ ozs. J. & J. Baldwin's "White Heather" Wheeling (or "Beehive" Double Knitting Wool) Four No. 8 Celluloid Knitting Needles with double points.

Cast on 100 stitches, 36 on one needle and 32 on to each of the other two needles.

Work, in rounds of ribbing (knit 2 and purl 2) for 3 inches.

Knit plain for 4 inches. Then repeat from the first round of decreasing in the Plain Helmet,—as described above.

M.T.

Patterns for a 'plain helmet', otherwise known as a balaclava, with a ribbed neck along with a sleeping helmet featured in a Baldwin's knitting booklet.

MITTENS

MATERIALS REQUIRED.—2½ ozs. (a little over ⅓ Cut) J. & J. BALDWIN'S 3 ply "White Heather" Wheeling (or Beehive Double Knitting Wool). Four No. 11 Knitting Needles.

Cast on 52 stitches (18 on each of two needles and 16 on the 3rd needle.)

Work, in rib of knit 2 and purl 2, for 36 rounds.

Knit 10 rounds in plain knitting.

47th round.—(Commence the thumb). Purl 1, increase once in the next stitch (by knitting through the loop just underneath the stitch). knit 2, increase once in the next stitch, purl 1, knit to the end of the round. The 2 purled stitches mark the outside of the thumb.

*Knit 2 rounds plain—while purling the stitches that were purled in the previous round.

50th round.—Increase once on the inside of each of the purled stitches, then knit plain to the end of the round.

Repeat from * until there are 18 stitches

between the 2 purled stitches.

Knit 2 more rounds without increasing ; then, in the next round, knit 1 (the purled stitch), put the next 18 stitches on to a thread and leave them for the thumb, cast on 4 stitches after the knit 1, follow on and finish the round.

Knit 10 rounds plain knitting.

Then knit 10 rounds, in rib of knit 2 and purl 2, and cast off loosely.

For the thumb take up the 18 stitches that were left on the thread and divide them on to two needles ; with the third needle knit up 6 stitches along the space between the two needles. Knit 6 rounds plain knitting.

Then knit 6 rounds, in rib of knit 2 and purl 2, and cast off loosely.

M.T.

BODY BELT
(IN RIBBING)

MATERIALS REQUIRED.—3¾ ozs. (1½ Cuts) J. & J. BALDWIN'S 5 ply "WHITE HEATHER" Scotch Fingering Wool. Two No. 10 and two No. 7 Celluloid Knitting Needles.

¶ The following instructions are for a belt knitted in two pieces, but, if preferred without a seam, simply commence with 200 stitches, on four needles, stocking fashion, while following the same general directions.

For one half cast 100 stitches on the No. 10 needles.

Work. in rib of knit 1 and purl 1, for 5 inches.

Then take the No. 7 needles and knit 7 more inches.

Cast off very loosely and sew up the two side seams neatly with the wool.

(The effect of using coarser needles for the last 7 inches is to give a rather greater width to the lower part of the belt. The tighter ribbing at the top then keeps the garment in position, and the absence of a correspondingly firm band at the lower edge prevents the latter from working up,—a point of great importance to the wearer's comfort).

M.T.

"WHITE HEATHER" FOR LUCK!

"WHITE HEATHER" SCOTCH FINGERING is soft to the touch and washes well. For a BODY BELT, so useful for preventing colic, either pure Undyed Natural (400½ shade), or White is best.

¶ For a rather lighter garment, 4 ply (50's) "WHITE HEATHER" Scotch Fingering may be used, while working to the same instructions. There will be no alteration in the actual size so long as the needles remain the same.

Baldwin's patterns for fingerless mittens and a body belt – designed to keep the midriff safe from chills.

NEW TRENCH HOSE.

THIS NEW HOSE will prove an immense boon for our soldiers at the front engaged in the trenches. They are intended for wearing with the long " gum " or rubber boots, and are made waterproof by soaking in linseed oil until thoroughly saturated. The oil is then squeezed out as tightly as possible and the stocking hung up to dry. This is generally accomplished in about forty-eight hours.

As the stockings are very easily and quickly knitted there is no reason why every man engaged on trench work should not be furnished with a pair, and so be protected against that awful malady known as frostbite. It cannot be too widely known that two pairs of socks should be worn by each man working in the trenches. With this stocking, which, by the way, goes over the ordinary sock, frostbite and " trench-foot " will be things of the past.

Trench hose – woolly leggings to be worn between socks and boots were soaked in linseed to give them waterproof properties.

Seven ounces of thick, fleecy wool with a set of No. 10 steel knitting needles will be required. Natural colour wool is best. Commence by casting 20 stitches on each of three needles and join round. Knit the first ribbing closely, but the remainder of the work should be done softly so that it may be thoroughly porous. For the ribbing k1, p1 alternately for 21 rows. When the stocking is in use this ribbing is turned down and keeps the stocking in place.

Knit plainly, without any back seam for fifty-four rows.—55th row. Knit 3, slip 1, knit 1, pass the slipped stitch over, knit 24, knit next 2 together, knit remainder of row. Knit six rows plain.—62nd row. Knit 4, slip 1, knit 1, pass the slipped stitch over, knit 22, knit 2 together, knit remainder plain. Knit six rows plain.—69th row. Knit 5, slip 1, knit 1, pass the slipped stitch over, knit 20, knit next 2 together, knit remainder plain.— Knit next six rows plain.—76th row. Knit 6, slip 1, knit 1, pass the slipped stitch over, knit 18, knit next 2 together, knit remainder plain.

The stitches in the round are now reduced to 52, that is, 16 on the first needle, 16 on the second, and 20 on the third. Knit the first needle, knit on the first needle the next 10 on the second needle. There are now 26 on the first needle. These are for the heel. Divide the remaining 26 equally between the other two needles. Knit 42 rounds plain.

Now on the first needle knit and purl alternate rows for the heel, 12 rows in all.—13th heel row. Knit 17, slip 1, knit 1, pass the slipped stitch over, turn.—14th row. Slip 1, purl to the 9th from the end, purl the 7th and 8th together, turn.—15th row. *Knit to the decreasing stitch, slip this, knit next stitch, pass the slipped stitch over, turn.—16th row. Slip 1, purl to the decreasing stitch, purl this and the following stitch together, turn and repeat from * until all the side stitches are taken in.

Raise and knit the stitches down the side of the heel, knit the front stitches all on one needle (26), take up and knit the stitches on this side of the heel and divide the heel stitches evenly on two needles. Knit around for two rows, then take over the first and last of the front stitches to the heel needles, thus leaving 24 for the front.

* On the first heel needle knit 1, slip 1, knit 1, pass the slipped stitch over, knit to within the last three on the second heel needle, knit the 3rd and 2nd together, knit 1* knit next two rows plain, then repeat the decreasing and following two rows plain until the heel stitches are reduced to 12 on each needle. Knit 26 rows plain.—27th row. *On the front needle knit 1, slip 1, knit 1, pass the slipped stitch over, knit to within 3 from the end, knit the 2nd and 3rd together, knit 1, knit 1 on next needle, slip 1, knit 1, pass the slipped stitch over, knit remainder plain, knit next needle to within 3 from the end, knit next 2 together, knit 1.

Knit 2 rows plain, * repeat from * twice more, then decrease in every second row three times, then in every row until only 8 stitches remain. Put these on two needles and knit 2 together, one from each needle, knit next 2, cast off, and so on till all are cast off. Fasten the thread and cut it. Bring the end of the thread through to the inside and darn it in neatly to prevent ripping.

The stocking is now ready for waterproofing. Place it in a shallow vessel and pour the oil over it, turn it a couple of times and allow it to soak, then squeeze out all the oil possible and hang up in a dry place where there is plenty of ventilation for a day or two until quite dry. Press with a warm iron when it will be ready for despatching to the front.

Measurement for the trench stocking illustrated : Ribbing, 4 inches ; width of stocking at top, 7 inches across, 14 inches round ; length from top of plain knitting to first decrease, 9 inches ; length from top of plain knitting to beginning of heel, 18 inches ; length of foot. 11¾ inches. These measurements are for the medium size.

FIRST
WORLD
WAR

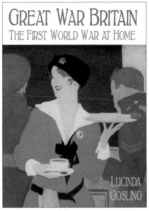

GREAT WAR BRITAIN
THE FIRST WORLD WAR AT HOME

LUCINDA
GOSLING

9780752491882

LUCY ADLINGTON

GREAT WAR FASHION

TALES FROM THE HISTORY WARDROBE

9780752493480

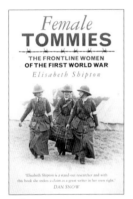

Female TOMMIES
THE FRONTLINE WOMEN OF THE FIRST WORLD WAR
Elisabeth Shipton

'Elisabeth Shipton is a stand-out researcher and with this book she stakes a claim as a great writer in her own right.'
DAN SNOW

9780752491431

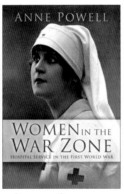

ANNE POWELL

WOMEN IN THE WAR ZONE
HOSPITAL SERVICE IN THE FIRST WORLD WAR

9780752493602

MILDRED ON THE MARNE
MILDRED ALDRICH FRONT-LINE WITNESS 1914–1918

DAVID SLATTERY-CHRISTY

9780752497686

THE WORKERS' WAR

BRITISH INDUSTRY AND THE FIRST WORLD WAR
ANTHONY BURTON

9780752498867

To explore these and all our commemorative titles visit:
www.thehistorypress.co.uk

The History Press